D1207220

THE ARCHITECT AS DEVELOPER

THE ARCHITECT

BY JOHN PORTMAN AND JONATHAN BARNETT

AS DEVELOPER

McGRAW-HILL BOOK COMPANY

NEW YORK   ST. LOUIS   SAN FRANCISCO   AUCKLAND   DÜSSELDORF   JOHANNESBURG

KUALA LUMPUR   LONDON   MEXICO   MONTREAL   NEW DELHI   PANAMA   PARIS   SÃO PAULO

SINGAPORE   SYDNEY   TOKYO   TORONTO

Library of Congress Cataloging in Publication Data

Portman, John Calvin.
    The architect as developer.

    1. Portman, John Calvin.   2. Architecture and
society—United States.   3. Cities and towns—
Planning—United States.   4. Real estate
investment.   I. Barnett, Jonathan, joint author.
II. Title.
NA737.P63B37   728.5   76-19062
ISBN 0-07-050536-5

2 3 4 5 6 7 8 9 0   HDHD   7 8 5 4 3 2 1 0 9 8 7

The editors for this book were Jeremy Robinson and Beatrice E. Eckes,
the designer was Jan White, and the production supervisor
was Frank P. Bellantoni. It was set in Aster
by York Graphic Services, Inc.

Printed and bound by Halliday Lithograph.

Part 1: Architecture

for buildings
people
use
every
day

Why John Portman became an entrepreneur as well as an architect

by Jonathan Barnett

Most buildings that win awards and are published in architectural magazines have been designed for situations in which finance is not the primary consideration: headquarters of major corporations, nonprofit institutions, prominent government offices, or the homes of wealthy people. Architects like to think that all buildings deserve the same care and attention that is lavished on these few special structures, but they are well aware that the architectural profession, for all its theories and aspirations, has had only a marginal influence on our everyday surroundings, which are formed by the real estate market, operating in a context of government regulation and public works construction. Architects are seldom consulted about building location, size, or use; and the assumptions that developers or government officials make about the budget tend to determine the structure and materials. All too often, the basic design concept becomes a matter of routine, leaving the architect to translate other people's decisions into technical drawings.

Even those architects who are famous for their talent, and will not touch a routine commission, must wait until they are called upon. Their role in shaping the environment has been a subsidiary one; they can do only what they are asked to do.

John Portman is an architect who can and does design the headquarters for a bank or a nonprofit institution, but he found the usual professional role to be too passive and too uncertain. Instead he became a real estate entrepreneur, developing projects and then hiring himself to design them. By doing so, he has been able to change the practice of both architecture and real estate. Portman's vision as a designer has seen possibilities in situations that look unpromising to conventional investors. At the same time, he has demonstrated that large and splendid spaces, which are usually found only in heavily subsidized institutional buildings, can be practical commercial investments.

The people who are drawn to the practice of architecture have quite different temperaments from those who are attracted to real estate, and the two professions are unreceptive to the subtleties of each other's work. The result is a lack of communication, to put it mildly. A developer may have creative investment ideas, but his assumptions about buildings are likely to be ordinary and stereotyped. The architect can devise unusual buildings, but he will not be able to assess their practicability as real estate. By controlling both architecture and development, Portman has found new ways to give amenity and coherence to our everyday environment.

Portman has learned to think of real estate architecturally, and architecture entrepreneurially.

What Portman calls the "coordinate unit" is a major factor in his approach to real estate development. The size of the unit is based on the distance that an average person is willing to walk without looking around for some form of transportation. The coordination comes from a way of thinking about an urban center that is analogous to the process of designing a building. There are certain functional elements, be they bedroom, living room, dining room, kitchen; or apartments, hotels, shops, and offices. All the elements need to be present, and they can be combined and arranged in various ways, some of which work better than others. If the design process is successful, the building—or urban center—will have an integrity of its own; it will be more than the coming together of its separate parts. Such coordination makes for better architecture; and a building that is a necessary element of an overall concept is also a better real estate investment.

Portman is very much aware that an interest in shaping the whole environment should not lead to designs that impose a narrow and arbitrary vision on a public that is looking for something quite different. His approach to environmental design is based on observations of the way people behave in public places. He tries to anticipate the psychological reaction of the building's ultimate user and plan accordingly. People can't walk into a Portman building and remain oblivious to their surroundings. They look up, startled by the large and unusual spaces; they explore; they try out the different experiences that the building offers.

Portman's desire to create an environment that is more responsive to the needs of the ordinary person grows quite naturally out of designing for commercial uses; and the marketplace, where success depends on attracting customers, operates as a check on Portman's ideas about what people want and need. The art of architecture and the practical necessities of real estate are not necessarily antagonistic.

All the same, Portman's work tends to make the traditional practitioners of both development and architecture uneasy.

The developer senses, correctly, that Portman's business purpose may be different from his own. Portman sees the financing of a building as a means toward a designed environment of value both to the public and to the investor. The largest immediate "bottom line" for the financial statement is not necessarily his goal. At the same time, other architects tend to bestow on Portman the same kind of suspicion that the literary world reserves for a best-selling novelist. Commercial success and art are not expected to go together.

The architectural profession has only gradually begun to understand how important Portman's example may prove to be. Not only has he been able to take a more active role in changing the environment, but he has solved, at least for himself, a problem that has beset architects and other artists since the end of the eighteenth century: how to replace the aristocratic patron who had traditionally made it possible for the architect to do his best work. Good buildings take more time and trouble than ordinary buildings and often more money as well. To create a fine work of architecture required a patron as well as a good architect: no Parthenon without Pericles, no Versailles without Louis XIV.

In these days of corporate decision making, fewer and fewer individuals have the power or the inclination to be patrons of architecture. Government and business leaders want to prove their fiscal responsibility and efficiency, not to be remembered as benefactors of the arts. Portman has found a way to be his own patron.

However, Portman is not a patron in the traditional sense. He did not begin his career as a wealthy man; his buildings have no resources beyond those available in an ordinary real estate deal. So his buildings must succeed in the marketplace. He had to master the process of real estate investment and turn it to his own purposes, and he had, by experiment, to create a new kind of business and professional organization.

Portman's innovations continue to lead him into unusual pathways of design and to opportunities at a larger and larger scale. Born in 1924 and working in areas where success generally comes late in life, Portman should have many years of productive work ahead of him. His ideas about architecture and investment are still evolving, and it is too soon for a verdict on his accomplishments, a judgment that, in any case, is a job for critics and historians.

The reason that Portman and I decided to write this book at this time is that we both believe that many urban and environmental problems will not be solved until an integrated design-development process—seeking lasting value, not quick profits—becomes the normal means of designing and building cities. We wish to put before real estate developers and investors, permanent lenders, government officials, design professionals, and the public the results of Portman's experience to date. We feel that his work demonstrates that designs which improve the quality of urban life can also be sound real estate investments.

In an earlier book[1] I described the experience that my colleagues and I in New York City have had with special zoning districts and other devices for promoting environmental design. Many of these measures were created in an adversary relationship with real estate developers, although the real estate community later came to see the advantages of some of our proposals.

I have followed Portman's work with great interest since I first met him in 1964, because he was approaching urban design from a complementary direction, using the techniques of real estate development to produce greater amenity for the public, out of conviction, not to comply with regulations. For such design concepts to become the norm, architects must learn to understand the mechanisms of real estate, and developers must become aware that the design process offers many alternatives to the usual development "package."

Real estate operations often depend on secrecy, and exact figures measuring the influence of the developer are hard to come by. However, it is possible to make some good guesses based on the statistics of building activity. We know that locations and designs of most new housing are determined by the real estate developer. According to the *Dodge/Sweet's Construction Outlook*, $63 billion was spent on building construction in 1975. Of this figure, $31.4 billion went for residential buildings: subdivisions of one- and two-family houses, garden apartments, and high-income apartment developments. Even some subsidized housing is built by developers under various government programs. In 1972, which was more representative of recent building construction, the total amount spent on all buildings was $69.4 billion, of which $43.1 billion went to residential construction. In 1975, $4.15 billion was expended for office buildings

[1]Jonathan Barnett, *Urban Design as Public Policy: Practical Methods for Improving Cities*, Architectural Record Books, McGraw-Hill Book Company, New York, 1974.

and $5.6 billion for stores and other commercial construction. These are both categories in which the developer accounts for most of what is built. The corresponding figures in 1972 were $4.8 billion and $6 billion. When you add in several billion dollars' worth of factories in developments organized by real estate speculators, an estimate ascribing two-thirds of all building to real estate developers looks quite conservative, and this estimate does not include government buildings and other structures whose size and locations are determined by real estate trends. Although the real estate industry is the major force shaping our surroundings, it has done little to recognize its responsibility to the environment. With some honorable and infrequent exceptions, developers have been selling the public a very inferior product. In our country, with its history of rapid growth and change, developers have had little trouble in marketing buildings of poor design, because any product has been better than none.

Architects on their side have often acted as if the subject of real estate finance should not be discussed in polite society. Real estate is not usually taught in architectural schools, there is very little about it on the architect's licensing examination, and the art historians who do so much to define architectural thought have very little to say about the social and economic forces that make most buildings possible.

The result of this taboo is that an architect often finds that he does not have a clear sense of whether or not his design is an appropriate answer to the developer's problem. He doesn't understand how different designs change the building's financial feasibility or its real estate market. He is left in the position of constantly experimenting to see what he can persuade his client to do. It is not surprising that developers tend to seek out those architects who stick to tried and true formulas and minimum building costs and fees.

The architectural profession has consoled itself by reflecting that a few special buildings can set a good example and raise the level of other buildings. There is some truth in this theory, but artistic concepts don't travel well when they are translated into an entirely different context. Eero Saarinen's design for the Gateway Arch in St. Louis becomes McDonald's golden arches; and the hoped-for style or vernacular that would raise the general level of architecture has never come to pass.

New external factors are forcing developers to do better work: stronger zoning regulations, design review boards, environmental legislation. Portman's design-development process suggests an alternative to such adversary requirements, one that is beneficial to the investor as well as to the public.

The purpose of this book is to explain the basic principles of Portman's designs and the procedures needed to implement them. We are not saying "Admire Portman's buildings"; we are saying "This is how Portman does it." All the same, the objective is to create fine works of architecture and a better environment; if the results are not worth the effort, then neither is the process. We hope that as many individuals and organizations as possible will be moved to emulate and improve upon Portman's work and that the result will be to make the surroundings in which we spend our daily lives more workable and more humane.

The tallest building in Atlanta, Georgia, is the seventy-story Peachtree Plaza Hotel, a cylindrical tower clad in mirror glass, with elevators in a tubular glass structure providing a spectacular journey up and down along its reflecting surface. This hotel is only one element of Peachtree Center, the prototype of Portman's coordinate unit, where all the buildings were designed and developed by John Portman and most are owned by Portman and his partners. There is a massive Merchandise Mart; and, nearby, there will be an associated Apparel Mart. There are five office buildings, a multilevel Shopping Gallery with a dinner theater on top, several parking garages, and another hotel, the Hyatt Regency Atlanta, marked on the skyline by its rooftop restaurant, which looks rather like a model of the planet Saturn.

It was this Hyatt hotel that was Portman's first conspicuous success as an architect-entrepreneur. The hotel is built around an exceptional indoor space, 120 feet on each side, which is surrounded by twenty-two floors of balcony-corridors that give access to the hotel rooms. The elevators have curved glass windows that look out into the main space, so that the journey to your hotel room provides the same sort of thrill as a ride in an amusement park. The revolving rooftop restaurant is reached by a similar elevator, which shoots you up through the roof and then through a glass-walled tube that gives you a glimpse of the surrounding city before you arrive at the Polaris Lounge, which does indeed feel as if it is orbiting above the hotel.

This combination of showmanship and authentic architectural grandeur was unique when Portman designed and developed it. The hotel was purchased by Hyatt while it was still under construction and proved enormously successful right away. Hyatt followed up this success by building a whole series of hotels that have many features in common with the Atlanta Regency. Portman designed two of them; the others were designed by different architects, who usually adopted the large interior courtyard, glass-enclosed elevators, and revolving rooftop restaurant used by Portman in Atlanta.

The Portman hotels attracted worldwide attention among architects, but they tend to be identified in the public mind with Hyatt, as the result of Hyatt's advertising, which features the buildings but generally doesn't mention who designed them.

Main space of the Hyatt Regency Atlanta at Peachtree Center, which became a new prototype for hotel design. The central enclosed court is 120 feet square and twenty-three stories high.

The ideas that Hyatt adopted and translated into a formula for hotel design represent only a small part of Portman's much more complex design philosophy. The impressive success of the Atlanta Regency hotel also has something to do with its position as part of a coordinate unit. Some of the demand for hotel rooms comes from the shows at the neighboring Merchandise Mart, and the hotel and its restaurants have an important relationship to the nearby office buildings and shops.

The heart of Peachtree Center is a group of four office towers that are placed symmetrically around two sunken courtyards and a structure that Portman calls the Shopping Gallery, a four-story space with a sloping glass roof that connects to the other buildings and provides frontage for shops at each level. One of the courtyards is next to the Little Mermaid restaurant. On a pleasant day, you can take a tray from the restaurant or a sandwich from one of the other shops in the center and eat beneath a yellow umbrella, looking up at the surrounding buildings through tree branches and trailing vines, or watching the ever-changing parade of your fellow diners. The second courtyard contains a fountain and is surrounded by the windows of the elegant Midnight Sun restaurant. There is another café in the Shopping Gallery, where potted trees and hanging plants beneath the sloping glass roof create a greenhouse atmosphere. Here diners can watch the people on the escalators leading to the different shopping levels or follow a constant stream of moving lights on the underside of the escalator structure, which symbolizes the movement of the escalators and greatly enlivens the scene.

The completion of the seventy-story hotel has given Peachtree Center

10

another focal space, which is symbolically the reverse of the spatial experience provided at the Hyatt Regency hotel. Instead of the rooms surrounding a large covered atrium, a compact tower containing the rooms comes down into the center of a seven-story public area. Below the intersection of the tower and roof, the rooms are removed, and only the supporting columns and the central elevator core come down to the ground, where, at the main lobby level, they stand in a sizable reflecting pool. Boat-shaped islands are pushed out between the columns, providing a variety of places to sit and sip a drink while looking at the people walking across the bridges that lead to the elevators or the balconies opposite. This space functions as both the hotel lobby and a second Peachtree Center shopping concourse, giving access to meeting rooms and restaurants and also to many specialty shops and Davison's department store, which is the next building south on Peachtree Street.

No functional element of Peachtree Center is unique. Rockefeller Center in New York is an older and larger office complex. Galleria Center in Houston and many suburban shopping centers have large indoor areas for stores and restaurants. What is special about Peachtree Center is the grandeur of the architectural spaces, the close coordination of all the elements, and the way in which the center helps to pull downtown Atlanta together.

Above, the garden courtyard of Peachtree Center, where you can bring your tray from the Little Mermaid restaurant or your own lunch in a brown paper bag. At right, the lake in the garden court of the Peachtree Plaza Hotel, the latest addition to Peachtree Center. Bridges connect the various levels of shops and convention rooms to the cylindrical hotel tower at left.

A system of bridges over streets and buildings will allow you to walk in a protected environment from Davison's to the Hyatt Regency or to the Apparel Mart, both several blocks away. This network is of equal value to hotel visitors and to the people who work downtown. Peachtree Center is also attracting shoppers and entertainment audiences from the Atlanta metropolitan area because it offers a range of services and an environment that can't be found in the suburbs. It is a little world of design and forethought with oases of space and of water, trees, and flowers in the aggregation of separate buildings that makes up most of downtown Atlanta. It is also a series of planned functional relationships: the interplay between visitors who come for the trade shows at the mart and the shops and department stores; the full range of restaurants, from takeout shops to elaborate gourmet dining; the dinner theater that brings people at night when the offices are closed.

Because Portman started with a single building, the Merchandise Mart, and only gradually found the means to build Peachtree Center up to its present size and scope, it is not as consistent architecturally as later Portman downtown designs. Peachtree Center has an air of improvisation and experiment: it is the place where Portman learned how to design groups of buildings and where he has tried out some of his more spectacular ideas.

Above, lunchtime at the café in Peachtree Center's Shopping Gallery.

Peachtree Center represents only a small portion of the work that Portman has done. His major projects include the four office buildings and hotel at the Embarcadero Center in San Francisco; the Renaissance Center in Detroit, which ultimately will contain twenty-three buildings, with a multilevel concourse connecting offices, a hotel, apartments, and shops; a merchandise mart and associated development at Porte d'Ivry, near Paris; a 30-acre suburban center in Cairo, Egypt; a prominent office building in Fort Worth; and a huge hotel and shopping concourse in Los Angeles.

The Fort Worth office building, like Portman's design for the Blue Cross–Blue Shield headquarters in Chattanooga, Tennessee, represents a situation in which development cost, although important, is not absolutely fundamental. All the other buildings named are real estate investments, in which building cost must be justified by income produced. Portman has a major interest in the Los Angeles, San Francisco, and Paris buildings, and his development firm is the managing partner in all three projects.

Portman has created an unusual combination of organizations to deal with his wide range of professional commitments, including not only an architectural and structural engineering office and a real estate development firm, but also management companies for properties he owns, the Merchandise Marts, the Midnight Sun Company, which runs the principal restaurants and the dinner theater in Peachtree Center, and Peachtree Purchasing, a firm that purchases well-designed furniture in bulk. Portman went into the restaurant business because he was sure that no outside concessionaire would produce the kind of atmosphere he had in mind or keep up his standards of food and maintenance once the restaurants were in operation. The purchasing firm gives Portman freedom in selecting furniture for the interiors he designs, because it can purchase in volume at prices that are competitive with conventional contract furniture.

The heart of Portman's empire is his office on the nineteenth floor of Peachtree Center South. It is spacious and quiet, the floor covered in a rich, chocolate brown carpet, the furniture a mixture of original Portmans and pieces by other designers, the lobby displaying some of Portman's art collection, whose catholicity might raise a few eyebrows in the New York art world. Portman's own office is a large, orderly space with windows on three sides. Placed on the center line of the interior wall is a desk that is usually covered with rows of the latest architectural magazines from all over the world, along with business and financial publications. A circular glass conference table stands at one side, and a group of upholstered furniture at the other. The surroundings are well calculated to convince a visiting businessman or investor that the owner of the office is a man of substance, while not denying Portman's taste or his vocation as a designer.

This nineteenth-floor office is primarily ceremonial, as Portman prefers to go to the part of the building where work is being done rather than have work brought to him. He takes a guiding role in every project in his office, from early financial and conceptual studies to the management of the completed building. It is not unusual for principals of architectural firms to do little design themselves; they preside

over a process in which the actual design is done by other hands. Portman, by contrast, sets the basic design concept for each building; he is involved in all the major decisions about arrangement, structure, and detail; and he designs the principal interior spaces himself, right down to the furniture and fixtures.

An open staircase connects the reception area of his office to John Portman and Associates, architects and engineers, on the floor below, and he spends a lot of his day going up and down that stair. At the same time, he is running a major property development business in which much of his time is necessarily given to financial matters that have no direct connection to design. He must also travel to his project offices in places like San Francisco, Los Angeles, Detroit, Brussels, Paris, and Cairo.

Naturally, he is very dependent on key staff members. While his organization is distinctly Portman-centric in nature, it would not be workable without a large group of capable people to assume important responsibilities. Portman's own time is very carefully guarded, as every minute of the day must be used to the utmost. He takes very few telephone calls, which are skillfully deflected; he attends no more meetings than are absolutely necessary; and he accepts few speaking engagements.

At left, the reception
area at Portman Proper-
ties, with the stair
that leads to Portman's
architectural office
on the floor below.
Above, Portman confers
in his office with
longtime associate
Stanley (Mickey) Stein-
berg. The desk, chairs,
conference table, and
light fixture are all
Portman designs.

One organization chart for all of Portman's operations would be something like a clock, a circle with Portman in the center and the various steps of what Portman calls the "building birth cycle" arranged chronologically. Portman Properties would occupy the space from noon to about four o'clock, followed by John Portman and Associates, the architectural office. Because much of the work in this office is generated by Portman Properties, there is some overlap of staff and function, and architectural design is considered much earlier in the "birth cycle" than is commonly the case. Assumptions are not made about land and financing until they have been tested against the design; market studies are based on an actual architectural concept; and cost estimates built into the financing are not rule-of-thumb or based on other structures but are derived from the design of the actual building. The architectural office is organized so that each separate building project occupies a separate location. Portman moves around the office following the progress of each job, working at the desks where the drawings are done. Many of Portman's designs require daring structures, and the architectural office has a large engineering component that he estimates has grown to be the largest structural engineering office in the Southeast.

In accordance with what has been the ethics of his profession, no Portman organization engages in building contracting, but his office is

Portman at work on a design problem with Irving Wiener, one of the architects in his office.

closely involved with supervision at all stages of the construction process. Around nine o'clock on our chart is the interior design section of the firm. However, when you visit one of Portman's buildings while it is under construction, you see that an unusual amount of the interior design is an integral part of the structure of the building—another result of a building process controlled by one mind from start to finish.

At about ten o'clock is Peachtree Purchasing, the organization set up to buy in quantity the kind of furniture Portman wants in his buildings. Peachtree Purchasing now has substantial outside business from other firms seeking professional buying capability and better-designed furniture at competitive prices.

At the end of the cycle is the Atlanta Merchandise Mart and the other mart corporations, the company that manages Peachtree Center, and the other operating entities for properties owned by Portman and his partners. Portman Properties also exercise a watchdog role over all these separately capitalized companies and partnerships.

Somewhere in the circle there must also be a place for Portman's civic activities. As the landlord of much of downtown Atlanta, he inevitably takes a leading role in the life of his home city. He has been the president of Central Atlanta Progress and is a member of the board of

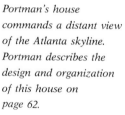

Portman's house commands a distant view of the Atlanta skyline. Portman describes the design and organization of this house on page 62.

the Atlanta Chamber of Commerce and of the Action Forum, an organization designed to foster cooperation between black and white interests in a city where the balance of power is shifting from one race to the other.

With such a full schedule, Portman tries to segregate travel, devoting about one week out of every four to a long journey that might take him from Atlanta to San Francisco to New York to Paris and then back to Atlanta.

Whenever possible, Portman will spend all day Saturday in the office. Without telephone calls or meetings, he is able to talk in a relaxed way with his assistants and spend hours at a time at the drafting table.

John and Jan Portman live quietly in a rather magnificent pavilion of Portman's own design on a hill in North Atlanta that commands a distant view of the skyline. They have six children, five sons and a daughter. Their oldest son, Michael, spent several years working for Portman Properties, and John C. III is an architect with John Portman and Associates. The Portmans are also preparing to build a summer house at Sea Island, and they maintain a suite at the top of the seventy-story hotel as a *pied-à-terre* and for business entertaining.

Portman's marts and real estate investments have given him financial

security, and he lives surrounded by the appurtenances of wealth and power. There is no question that he enjoys them and the fact that he has been able to give them to his family, but they are really a by-product. Portman's ambitions are elsewhere. He does not live ostentatiously, taking no part in the "jet set." The force that drives him through six- and seven-day weeks, recurring grueling travel, and constant attention to detail is the desire to be a great architect and to reshape cities. He looks at the money generated by his buildings as poker chips, the means to stay in the game. "I'm not rich," he will say. "I would be rich only if I stopped." Portman's middle name is not Calvin for nothing.

In 1953 Portman had just opened a one-room architectural office. He had no idea where the commissions would come from to keep his office going, and he had no capital beyond an ordinary savings account. How did he go from that uncertain existence to the position he occupies today? How did he develop the skills and the confidence needed to make this difficult transition?

The answer goes back to Portman's days in the late 1940s as a student at the Georgia Institute of Technology, where he was already known as a promising designer. One strong influence was Frank Lloyd Wright, who came to Georgia Tech as a visiting lecturer and had a profound effect on the direction of Portman's thinking. Wright regarded architecture as a comprehensive discipline that should give shape and direction to all aspects of life. Although he adopted the role of a maverick and social critic, every building that Wright designed was part of a utopian vision that was national in scale. Wright introduced Portman to comprehensive systems of social thought and to the study of philosophy, recommending that he pay particular attention to Emerson. Some of Emerson's self-confident optimism is clearly reflected in Portman's statements and actions, along with the Wrightian belief that the mission of architecture is to make a better world.

It is also clear from Portman's later work that he has made a thorough study of Wright's buildings, not so much of the details of external appearance as of their systems of organization, use of structure, and Wright's concept of organic unity as a design ideal. This direct influence from Wright distinguishes Portman's buildings from the work of most of his contemporaries, who have absorbed Wright's ideas in the more mechanistic form in which they were reinterpreted by his European followers.

Another important formative influence came from Portman's part-time work, while he was still a student, for the New York architects Ketchum, Gina and Sharp, who were associated in Atlanta with a local firm, H. M. Heatly, architects. Ketchum, Gina and Sharp were leading designers of department stores and other kinds of shops. Store design uses psychology in a very practical way. A buyer who intends to acquire a refrigerator or another "big ticket" purchase must invariably run the gantlet of impulse items: perfume, cosmetics, jewelry, gloves, neckties, and so forth. The arrangement of stores anticipates the buyer's reactions, and every step of the various possible journeys through the space is carefully studied. This experience with Ketchum, Gina and Sharp started Portman thinking about the reactions of people to their environment and led him to develop the observations about behavior that are the basis of his design philosophy. His work with store interiors also heightened his interest in lighting, cabinetwork, and the detailing of furniture. Portman takes a much greater interest in designing and detailing interiors than most architects do.

After architectural school, Portman worked for three years at Stevens and Wilkinson. This major Atlanta firm receives a great number of important and diverse commissions and makes a policy of hiring able designers and giving them many opportunities. Portman was able to try his hand at a number of important buildings and to follow them through the working-drawing process, an experience that enabled him to build up confidence in his abilities.

As soon as he had completed the three years of professional experience required for registration and had received his license, Portman opened his own office. He was so anxious for independence that he did not wait for any sure prospects, and the pace of his small office proved to be quite a comedown from the busy and successful Stevens and Wilkinson. Impatient and not content with the small-house projects and schoolroom additions that came his way, Portman began to think about real estate development as a means of producing architectural commissions. He had become friendly with Robert Wilby, a prominent Atlanta executive, while he was working at Stevens and Wilkinson on the headquarters of the Wilby, Kinsey Company. Wilby gave Portman an introduction to the late John O. Chiles, president of the Adams-Cates Company and one of the leading real estate men in Atlanta. Portman went to Chiles with a proposition: Portman would be willing to give Adams-Cates some architectural advice, if Adams-Cates in turn would permit him to observe a number of real estate projects.

Intrigued, Chiles agreed. Portman was able to go to meetings and see how things were done; he became conversant with the basic elements of real estate development. Chiles, in turn, became favorably impressed with Portman. Chiles was later to play an important part in assembling the land for Peachtree Center and an even more decisive role in financing the first Peachtree Center hotel, with its highly unconventional architecture.

The Atlanta Merchandise Mart in 1961, before any of the other Peachtree Center buildings had been constructed. The mart has since been enlarged to twice the size shown, an expansion that had been provided for in the original plans.

Portman's initial venture into real estate was a proposed medical office building, developed in partnership with a small local real estate firm; but after a year of effort not enough tenants had signed up for the deal to go ahead. Portman found that he was out of pocket by about $7,500, which it would take him some time to pay back. He was able to send the drawings to the annual competition run by *Progressive Architecture* magazine, in which the building won an award—as Portman says, an architectural success but a promotional failure.

From his experience with the medical building, Portman concluded that in the future he would keep control of both the real estate and the architectural aspects of any project; he was not going to depend on someone else. He did not conclude that architects ought to stay out of real estate. If he was going to spend part of his time promoting real estate ventures, he realized that he would need help in carrying on his architectural practice. Because he did not have enough work to hire the necessary additional staff, he decided to approach Griffith Edwards and suggest that they combine their two firms. Portman calls this one of the best decisions of his life. Edwards was a professor at Georgia Tech and a nationally known authority on construction specification. About twenty years older, he had been one of Portman's teachers, and he had a well-established small practice.

The firm of Edwards and Portman was formed in 1956. Although each partner had agreed that either one could terminate the association on a month's notice, the partnership continued until 1969, when Edwards retired because of ill health. Edwards died in 1972. Edwards handled the administrative and construction side of the practice, leaving Portman free to design and to become involved in promotional ventures.

The most important of these ventures was the Atlanta Merchandise Mart, which was the means by which Portman got into real estate development on a large scale. Its success, like that of many such undertakings, was due in part to luck and good timing and in larger part to persistence and hard work. This is the story as Portman tells it:

The project began as a furniture mart; in fact, it really began as an attempt to get an architectural commission from Al Hendley. Mr. Hendley was the trustee for the Belle Isle Estate, which owned an old garage that the government had taken over toward the end of World War II for use by the Veterans Administration. I had learned that the VA was moving out into better quarters, thanks to a tip from my father, who was with the General Services Administration at the time. In 1942, while I was going to Tech High School, I worked part time parking cars in the Belle Isle Garage, and I knew the building intimately. I came up with the idea that it would make a great exhibition space, because you would have to do very little to convert the existing structure to this use.

So I went in to talk Mr. Hendley into turning the building into a permanent exhibition place, a merchandise mart, with Edwards and Portman as his architects.

Mr. Hendley said: "Young man, we've been in the U-Drive It, taxicab, and garage business all our lives, and we're too old to go into something we know nothing about. I've been planning on turning the building back into a garage; but I really don't want to do it, because there will be an awful lot of headaches and problems. I'd much rather lease it to someone and let him worry about what to do with it. I'll tell you what I'll do: you go out and form a corporation, and I'll lease the building to you. Then you can make it a mart or anything else you want."

So I said, "Thank you," and walked out. But the more I thought about it, the more I felt that leasing the Belle Isle Building might not be such a dumb idea. I started to talk to people around Atlanta. I met Randy Macon, whose father had once tried to put together a furniture mart. I had thought that Randy might have some of his father's files or records. There weren't any files, but Randy was working as a manufacturer's representative for the Williams Furniture Company, and he knew the business from that point of view. So he came in with me. We needed a man to go on the road and seek tenants; so I thought of John La Rue, who had been to architectural school with me and was a product salesman. So I asked John if he would be interested in getting involved with this thing in a promotional way. We also added a fourth partner, Herbert Martin, who had been with me at the Naval Academy Prep School and the Naval Academy during the war. He had experience working with trade shows as an assistant manager of a local hotel.

And that was how we formed our corporation. We each had equal shares, as there was nothing to share; but I was the president of the mart because it was my idea and I had recruited the others.

So we went to High Point, North Carolina, to the furniture shows, and started calling on manufacturers. In the meantime, I worked out a scheme for renting part of the Belle Isle Building from Al Hendley. The whole building had about 240,000 square feet in it, and we could only use 40,000 to start with. So I worked out a plan that took the front half of the first four floors for the mart; the rest of the structure could be operated as a garage.

Soon after we opened, we expanded to fill the whole top floor. Then we came down and filled the next floor, slowly pushing the garage out of the building. As things turned out, the mart filled the whole structure within a year after the opening.

The furniture mart was so successful that we realized there was a demand for a much larger building; we estimated that we could ulti-

mately fill 2 million square feet of display space and offices.

The Belle Isle Building was within walking distance of all the major hotel rooms in Atlanta at that time, and it became apparent that a downtown location had been a principal factor in our success. When we showed five alternative sites to potential mortgage lenders, they all told us that the plot at the corner of Peachtree and Harris Streets would be the best. This was the largest piece of land in single ownership in downtown Atlanta. It sold for the largest price that had been paid for a piece of property in the history of Atlanta.

Of course, what we had to start with was an option to purchase. This was before the decentralization of marketing in the United States. We were talking about a special-purpose building type in a location where such a building had never been done before. The lenders were very skeptical.

We had another problem: competition from others to build the mart. A well-established Atlanta developer by the name of Robert Holder had had great success in developing the Peachtree Industrial Boulevard, which was the biggest industrial development in the city at that time, and was doing very well. He had acquired a lot of property out in Gwinnett County, which was about 20 miles from downtown Atlanta, and proposed to build the mart there. It became quite a struggle between our group and his group as to who would be able to build, because there could be but one mart.

They were the proven developers, they had a board of directors on which substantial local people were involved, and they made a big effort to create the impression that we were just young guys out in left field.

When the Gwinnett County group couldn't raise the money they needed, they came very close to persuading the state that it should take over their mart project and build it under a public authority. Fortunately, Mills Lane, the president of the C. & S. Bank, convinced the key people in the state government that there was no point in spending public money on a project that could be done perfectly well by conventional means.

Things started moving our way when we received a mortgage commitment from Metropolitan Life, after its loan officer, Larry Benway, had come to town and gone through our operation in the Belle Isle Building. A major local landowner and developer, Ben Massell, agreed to buy the land and provide the additional equity that we needed.

Without Ben Massell the mart would never have been built. I later came to refer to him as Uncle Ben out of admiration, respect, and affection. He was a brilliant man, and working with him made a significant contribution to my development.

Looking back, I can see that another decisive advantage was our downtown location, within walking distance of all the existing hotels, department stores, restaurants, and other amenities that out-of-town people like. This was at a time when a lot of people were saying that downtown Atlanta was finished and that all major growth was going to take place in the suburbs. But we knew that no one wanted to drive 20 miles each way from his hotel out to Gwinnett County.

We broke ground for the mart in 1959 and were in the building by July

1961. The mart proved to be successful from the first. Ben Massell had given us an option to buy him out with a down payment and a second mortgage, provided we could come up with the money during the second year of the mart's operation. The mart did so well that we were able to exercise the option.

Portman had accomplished his original aim, using real estate development to provide a commission for his architectural firm. He also found himself the president and a principal shareholder of a successful business. But his ambitions were becoming larger; he began to formulate new and much more difficult goals for himself.

At this time, Portman was invited to the opening ceremonies at Brasília, the new capital of Brazil, which had been completely designed by architects and planners in accordance with what were then considered the most advanced principles of architecture and city design. Brasília's failures as an urban environment are well known. Portman concluded immediately that what was wrong was not the fault of the architects and planners but the result of basic errors in the theory of modern design. He came back to Atlanta with a new interest in the large-scale problems of city planning and a need to question all the principles of modern architecture that he had previously taken more or less for granted.

While Portman was making plans for Peachtree Center, a coordinated development for downtown Atlanta with the mart as the keystone, and as he worked on the designs of his own house and of such buildings as the Fine Arts Center at Agnes Scott College, he began formulating a consistent view of architecture which he calls his architectural philosophy.

Portman has a horror of being told what to think or do by critics and theorists or of becoming the follower of one or another school of design. He wants his achievements or his mistakes to be his own. At the same time, he is an avid reader of architectural books and magazines and has studied the work of Mies van der Rohe and Le Corbusier, as well as having a strong interest in Frank Lloyd Wright. Portman's work also gives indications that he was not unaware of the ways in which Eero Saarinen and Paul Rudolph were trying to solve similar problems, although he is very uncomfortable with any attempt to trace the influence of other architects in his buildings.

The first Peachtree Center office building provides an example of the steps by which Portman began to master the art of architecture and the craft of real estate development. This building marks the entrance of an important new actor in the story of Portman's development, the Dallas real estate investor Trammell Crow. Crow and Portman had met while Portman was developing the Merchandise Mart and Crow was building a similar venture in Dallas. After the Atlanta mart was completed, Crow and Portman bought out the shares of the other partners until each ended up owning half of the mart corporation. The Crow organization was a partner in several subsequent Portman developments, including other Peachtree Center buildings, a shopping center in suburban Atlanta, the Embarcadero Center in San Francisco, and the Merchandise Mart in Brussels.

26

Portman and Crow acquired control over two properties just to the south of the mart along Peachtree Street. They bought one of the parcels outright, but the second, much larger plot could be obtained only on the basis of a long-term lease. The trust department of the local bank that oversaw the property stipulated that at the end of the lease's ninety-nine years it should be possible to separate the main portion of the office building, which stood on its property, from the part that occupied the adjacent lot.

Portman's design for the office building expresses this constraint; not only is the southern 30 feet of the building detachable, but it is seen to be detachable. The central part of the office tower has the conventional arrangement of elevators, fire stairs, and utility ducts, surrounded by office space, but it is flanked on both sides by 30-foot-wide wings that are offset from the central core. The arrangement has the advantage of minimizing the apparent bulk of the office building and reducing the awkwardness of its juxtaposition to the mass of the Merchandise Mart, a relationship which had not been anticipated when the mart was designed. The design also has a useful side effect of multiplying the number of desirable corner offices. The dimensions of the curtain wall for the office building were picked up from the mart to provide as much congruity as possible.

The split real estate parcels suggested the building's three-part organization, but the form Portman adopted bears a strong resemblance to a building in Düsseldorf, the headquarters of the Phoenix-Rheinrohr Company, by two German architects, Helmut Hentrich and Hubert Petschnigg. This building was completed in 1960 and published in various architectural magazines around the time that Portman was designing 230 Peachtree Street. Did it influence him? Portman says no; he has no recollection of seeing it, and he arrived at his own conclusions independently.

In any event, the vocabulary established by this office building, offset masses and concrete curtain wall, has been followed by Portman in all the succeeding structures at Peachtree Center. He would much rather have experimented with new ideas, but he reasons that congruity for the whole complex is the most important design objective. The office buildings at the Embarcadero Center in San Francisco have a somewhat analogous design vocabulary, with the mass subdivided even further, because the purpose is similar: to minimize the effect of the building's bulk and its juxtaposition with other structures. The design of 230 Peachtree Street also makes a modest beginning in the use of urban open space, defined by sculpture and planting, which was to become a major theme of Portman's subsequent development.

Portman's own house had been completed by about this time, allowing him to see some of the elements of his newly formulated architectural philosophy in a fully realized form. He explains the importance that the design of this house had for him, beginning on page 62. His experience with his house had an immediate effect on his other work.

The mart was creating a demand for more hotel rooms in downtown Atlanta, and Portman decided to add a hotel to the complex of buildings he was creating. In partnership with a local investment

Above, the Phoenix-Rheinrohr Building in Düsseldorf, by Helmut Hentrich and Hubert Petschnigg. Below, Portman's Merchandise Mart and 230 Peachtree Street buildings, as seen from a bridge leading to a parking garage.

Portman's first design for the site of what is now the Hyatt Regency Atlanta hotel. The arrangement of the hotel rooms is conventional; there is no interior court.

One of two interior courtyards of the Antoine Graves Houses, low-income housing for the elderly, designed by Portman just before he began to work on the hotel.

company he obtained a ninety-nine-year ground lease on a substantial parcel diagonally opposite the mart on the other side of Peachtree Street. Portman's early schemes for this hotel were conventional: a podium containing the lobby, restaurants, convention meeting rooms, and other public spaces, with the hotel rooms as a tower on top.

During the design of this building, however, Portman made a decisive break with the usual way of designing hotels. He had recently completed some publicly aided housing for the elderly, the Antoine Graves Houses. In this building he had grouped the small apartments for the elderly, which are not unlike hotel rooms, around two interior courtyards. Each apartment was reached from a balcony-corridor that looked into one of the two courts, providing a sense of community and some sheltered interior spaces that could actually be used for communal purposes. The apartments have windows looking out on the court, so that each unit enjoys through ventilation. This design had turned out to be economic, even within the cost constraints of low-income housing, and Portman resolved to try something like it in his new hotel.

Shakespeare's Globe Theater was based on the design of a traditional coaching inn, with its octagonal courtyard, and many nineteenth-century hotels have interior courtyards, like that of the Brown Palace Hotel in Denver. But modern hotel design had become a cut-and-dried affair, with the ingenuity of the architects employed in shaving room sizes and material costs and not in creating grand public spaces.

Portman's design was thus a dramatic departure from accepted practice as well as a spreading of wings. For the first time he made use of his position as both architect and entrepreneur to try a design that would be possible only if both elements agreed. Here is what Portman says about the process of creating this building:

I didn't want the hotel to be just another set of bedrooms. The typical central-city hotel had always been a cramped thing with a narrow entranceway, a dull and dreary lobby for registration, elevators over in a corner, a closed elevator cab, a dimly lighted corridor, a nondescript doorway, and a hotel room with a bed, a chair, and a hole in the outside wall. That was the central-city hotel. I wanted to do something in total opposition to all this. I wanted to explode the hotel; to open it up; to create a grandeur of space, almost a resort, in the center of the city. The whole idea was to open everthing up; take the hotel from its closed, tight position and explode it; take the elevators and literally pull them out of the walls and let them become an experience within themselves, let them become a giant kinetic sculpture.

My partners in developing the hotel were a local real estate firm called the Phoenix Investment Company and an investor from Dallas named Fritz Hahn. Trammell Crow bought out Hahn's interest before construction began. Naturally, my partners were somewhat surprised by my design, but they agreed to go along with me and see if we could obtain financing. The man who deserves the credit for financing the hotel was the late John O. Chiles, the president of the Adams-Cates Company in Atlanta, who was successful in getting a mortgage commitment from the Massachusetts Mutual Life Insurance Company. John O. Chiles used to refer to me back in the late fifties as the Mari-

28

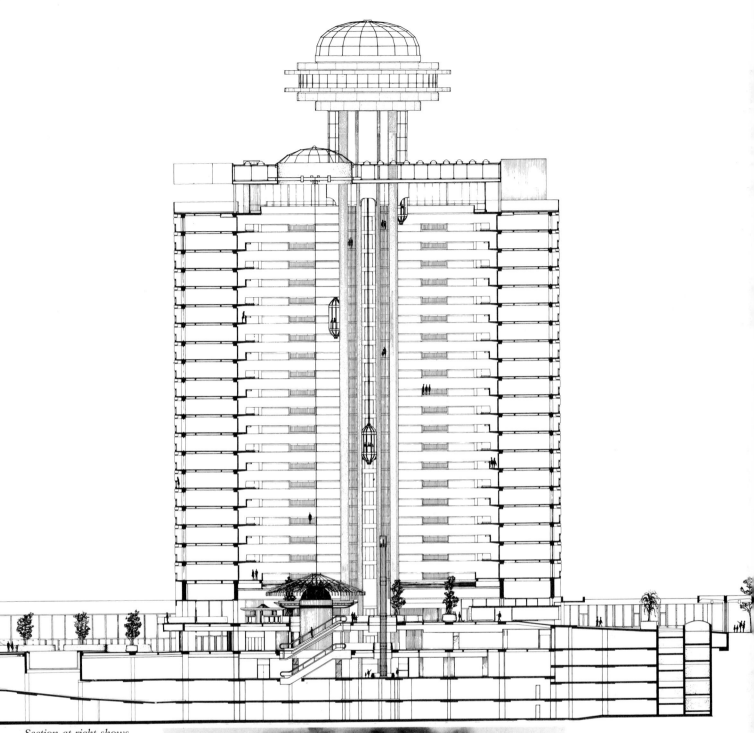

Section at right shows an early version of the hotel's interior court. Section above, which is taken looking in the opposite direction, shows the fully elaborated design.

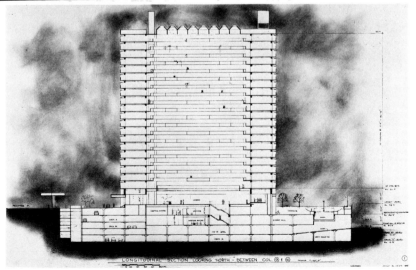

juana Kid. That was before marijuana was so widely known. He thought I was in outer space. All the same, he had a lot of confidence in me; and he was able to convince the people involved that if you were going to build another hotel in downtown Atlanta, it shouldn't be an ordinary building. When people came to Atlanta, we wanted them to try to get into our hotel first; its uniqueness would be its competitive advantage.

Everybody's first reaction was that this kind of hotel would cost a fortune, but you must remember that there are many ways to spend money. There is no fancy marble or terrazzo in this hotel; it's all concrete. The carpet, furniture, and fittings are as luxurious as those of any other hotel, but everything else is simple, conventional construction, using a minimum of materials. The money saved by avoiding fancy finishes and the saving in labor are what pay for the big space.

Now that many hotels with big interior spaces have been built, investors understand the cost trade-offs, but back then no one had ever seen a hotel like this before. I think my proposal was taken much more seriously because I had already been successful with the Merchandise Mart, and many people had not thought that it would work out either. If the hotel had been the first thing I ever did as a developer, the odds on getting it built would have been minimal.

However, during construction we had a run of bad luck. We had seven separate strikes, which added a year to the construction time and over $1 million in interest charges to the construction financing. Then, when the building was about four stories up, the Phoenix Investment Company got a new president, Richard Sorensen, who had been with a chain store. He didn't think that Phoenix should be in the hotel business. He asserted that what he knew was shopping centers, and he wanted to stay with a business that he understood.

Since the Phoenix Investment Company owned two-thirds of the hotel company, we either had to buy it out, which I couldn't do, or go along with the sale. We invited Conrad Hilton down and gave a big luncheon for him on top of the Merchandise Mart, out on the roof deck so that he could look over the site. We had all the investors there, and Hilton said: "That concrete monster will never fly." From then on, you can imagine that the other investors were really anxious to get rid of that hotel.

After talking to Hilton, Sheraton, Loews, and Western, we finally sold the hotel to the Hyatt House Corporation, which had a chain of motels on the West Coast. They had never owned a big downtown hotel up to this time. That they were willing to make this move is due to the vision of the late Donald Pritzker and his uncle Jack and to their excitement about the possibilities. They came to Atlanta and immediately wanted to make a deal, and we made one fairly quickly.

The hotel opened to tremendous response from the public, to great success. It launched the Hyatt House chain into the big leagues and created the position that they now hold in the hotel industry as one of the largest chains in the United States. The Regency has run about 85 percent occupancy and above since it opened, which is a very unusual figure for a downtown hotel. I was so confident in the success of the Regency that I bet Donald Pritzker $1,000 to a cup of coffee that it

Photograph of
the main space of
Peachtree Center,
taken from the
terrace of the
dinner theater.
All the buildings
in view were
designed and
developed by
Portman.

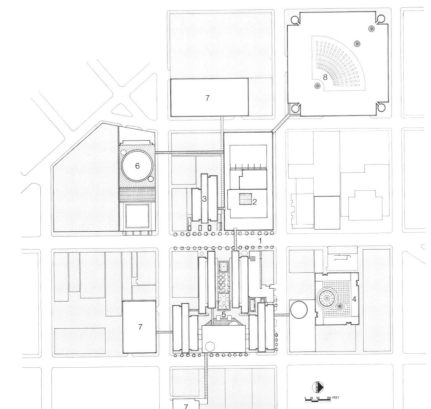

Site plan shows Peach-
tree Center today:
(1) Peachtree Street;
(2) the Merchandise Mart;
(3) the first Peachtree
Center office building;
(4) the Hyatt Regency
Atlanta hotel;
(5) the main Peachtree
Center office complex,
courtyards, Shopping
Gallery, and dinner
theater; (6) the Peach-
tree Plaza Hotel;
(7) parking garages; and
(8) the Apparel Mart.

would be doing over 90 percent occupancy within three months after opening. Three months after opening, the hotel was doing 94.6 percent; so that was a bet I won.

After the hotel, the next move in the growth of Peachtree Center was Portman's acquisition of a leasehold interest in the Whitehead Estate, about 2 acres of land directly across Peachtree Street from the first office building. This property, with additional land acquired later, gave Portman the opportunity to create the coordinated group of four office buildings around the courtyards and the multilevel shopping complex.

The most recent of these buildings was not completed until ten years after the first, but the use of a consistent design vocabulary based on

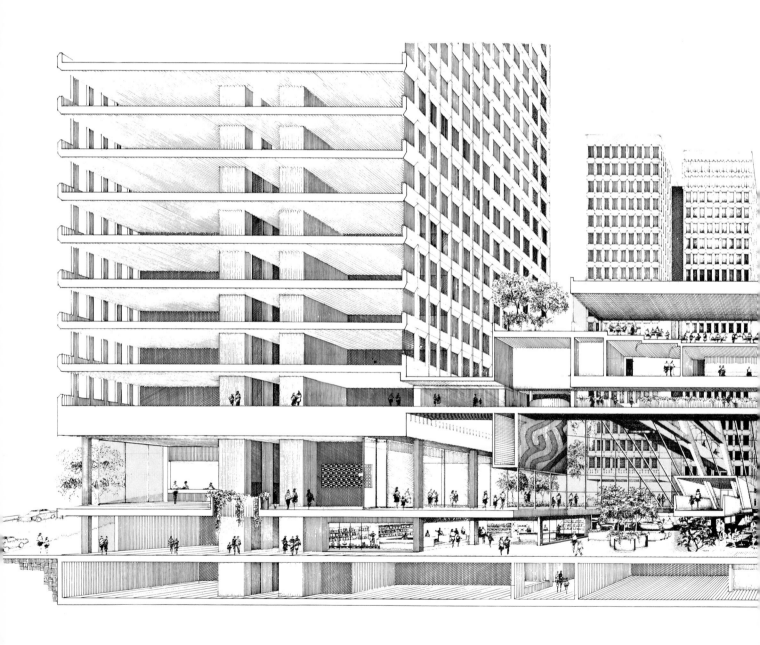

*Section perspective of
Peachtree Center looking
to the west from a van-
tage point somewhat sim-
ilar to the photograph
on the following page.   The
drawing shows the
relationship of the
various levels, the
position of the dinner
theater which draws
people through the
Shopping Gallery, and
the way in which
all the buildings are
pulled together into
a single entity.*

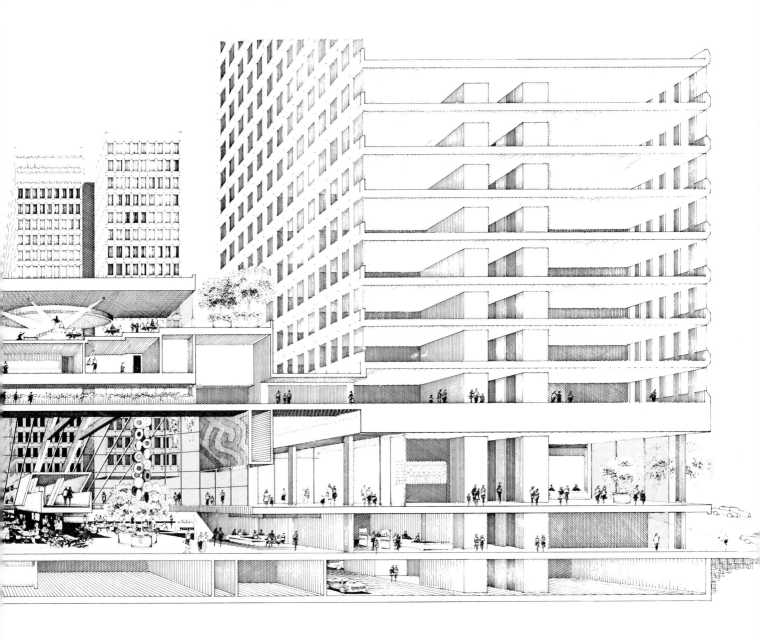

Top, the dinner theater set up for lunch and a matinee. Louvered blinds at windows are closed during a performance. Left, the bridge connecting the Shopping Gallery to the Franklin Simon store, which occupies a floor in one of the office buildings. Below, Peachtree Center at street level.

the first Peachtree office tower gives them an impressive unity. The consistency is more than superficial. Tenants, including Portman's own office, are able to expand horizontally by bridges from building to building, because the floor heights are uniform.

The shopping complex on the eastern side of this group of buildings is a vivid illustration of Portman's method of using architecture to affect real estate marketability. A dead-end location off a section of Peachtree Street that was not a strong shopping area in any case has become a major retail center.

Photograph, below, is taken inside the Shopping Gallery looking west.

The success is due partly to the proximity of major hotels and office buildings but clearly also to the fact that the space itself is attractive. If you build an interesting and pleasant place, people will use it.

Portman's first use of a cylindrical building for hotel rooms was the addition to the Hyatt Regency Atlanta. At right, the Peachtree Plaza, in which the whole hotel is a cylinder.

The Shopping Gallery has a dinner theater on top, added by Portman as an afterthought when he realized that the rooftop park he planned would be dead at night and the building would not be tall enough to enclose the space in the way that he felt it should be enclosed. The theater adds another kind of activity and helps draw people into the center at night, but Portman the developer found a way to put it there because Portman the architect thought it would be an improvement.

Portman's original design for Peachtree Center, as described in an architectural model that was kept in a small private room near his office, called for a tall office building across the street to the east of the courtyard, in something like the same position that the RCA Building occupies at Rockefeller Center. It was after he found himself unable to assemble this land that the shopping concourse and dinner theater were used to close the space instead. As an alternative to expanding to the east, Portman interests leased the old Henry Grady Hotel site on Peachtree Street, which permitted his center to expand southward, toward Atlanta's traditional business district.

Atlanta as a city has worked hard to make itself a convention center. It now stands third, after New York and Chicago, in numbers of convention visitors each year, and has just completed a new convention center of 450,000 square feet. The building on the Henry Grady site became a 1,120-room convention hotel, cylindrical in shape and seventy stories high. (The whole process of planning, designing, and building this hotel is described on page 156.)

The decision to build a hotel was not based on the marketability of hotel rooms alone but on the marketability of the design and its relationship with the rest of Peachtree Center, a place for customers at the mart to stay and a source of business for the shops and restaurants.

There are architectural models of apartment houses in the secret room where Portman has stored some of the designs for the ultimate growth of Peachtree Center, but thus far the market has not favored their being built. Residences would help to complete the coordinate unit, providing a balanced spectrum of land uses and keeping the center lively all day long. For the moment, the hotel population of transients gives some of the balance that full-time residents will one day provide and supports the restaurants and entertainment that operate at night.

The decision to use a cylindrical arrangement of hotel rooms in the second Peachtree Center hotel came out of the problem at hand, but it also repeated a motif that Portman has used a number of times in the past.

The first cylinder of hotel rooms was an addition to the original Hyatt Regency Atlanta. Successful beyond even Portman's most optimistic projections, the hotel needed more rooms from the day it opened, and the only possible place for them was a 50-foot sliver of land immediately next door. In order to get 200 hotel rooms onto the site, it was necessary to cantilever them over the existing hotel ballroom, and a cylindrical tower covered in reflecting glass was the most economical and least obtrusive addition that Portman could devise.

Portman's original design for the Hyatt hotel near O'Hare International Airport in Chicago had two interlocking atria, which spread the building over a large area. When this design proved inefficient, Portman turned to the cylindrical room arrangement again, using a single atrium with cylinders at the four corners, which produced the required number of rooms while staying within the Federal Aviation Administration height limitations.

In his big hotel for Los Angeles, Portman evolved a building composed of five cylindrical components. A major reason for doing this was that the hotel occupied an isolated site in the middle of an urban renewal district. The cluster of cylinders was the only group of forms that he felt would relate equally well to all the surrounding rectangu-

*In the Hyatt Regency
O'Hare, in Chicago, top,
Portman used a cylindri-
cal grouping of rooms
at the four corners.
The 1,500-room Bonaventure
Hotel in Los Angeles, bottom,
is a complex of five
cylindrical towers,
and the hotel tower
at the Renaissance Center
in Detroit, center, is
a seventy-story
cylinder similar to
the Peachtree Plaza in
Atlanta.*

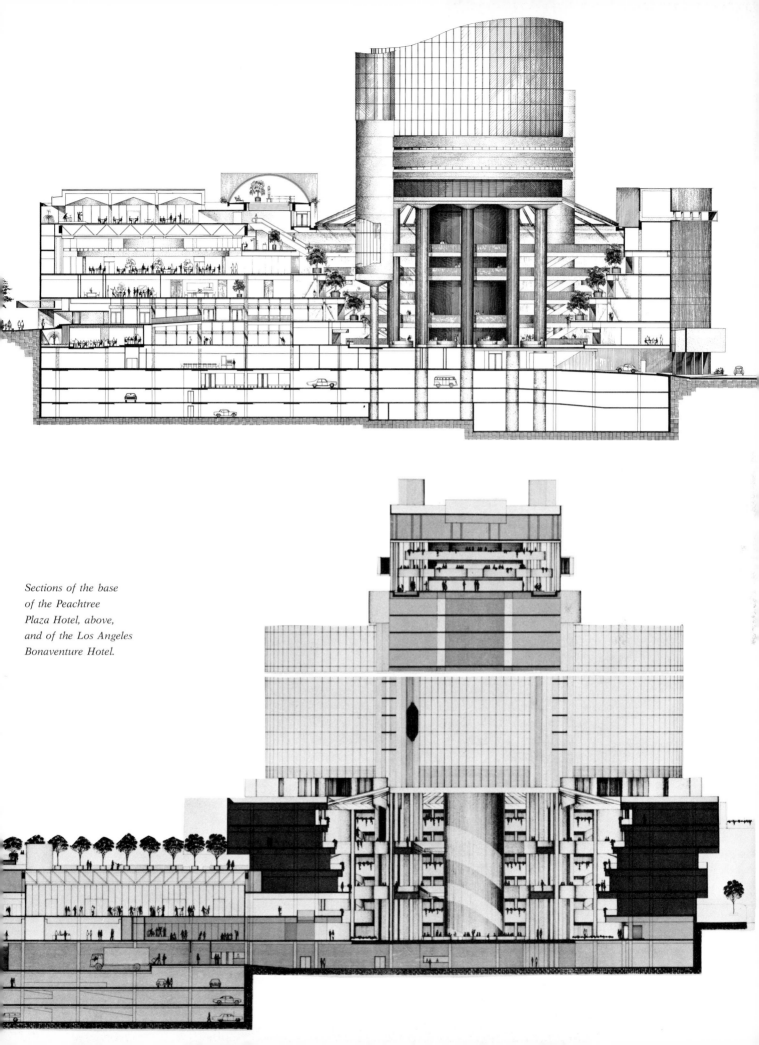

Sections of the base of the Peachtree Plaza Hotel, above, and of the Los Angeles Bonaventure Hotel.

lar buildings and help him to make the hotel a unifying element for the whole complex. In Detroit, for Renaissance Center, the hotel again became a single cylinder, but surrounded by four octagonal office buildings that form a cluster rather like the Los Angeles hotel but on a larger scale.

Portman is emphatic that this evolution of cylindrical building forms is not the development of a vocabulary of stereotypes but a series of responses to different sets of conditions. His proposed hotel for Times Square in New York, designed at much the same time as the Atlanta cylinder, is entirely different: a seven-story shopping mall and a thirty-four-story atrium enclosed by two parallel slabs of hotel rooms connected by bridges.

Portman's proposed Times Square hotel would have two large interior spaces, one for the seven floors of shops and the other for the hotel itself.

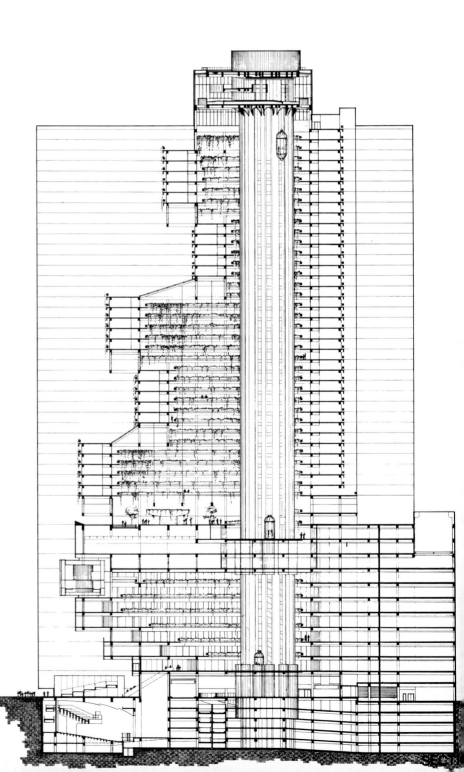

Below, the Merchandise
Mart in Brussels, designed
by Portman and developed
by Portman and Trammell
Crow. Portman's Apparel
Mart at Peachtree Center,
above, will have a com-
parable central space.

The circular floor plan for a hotel has certain natural advantages. It has relatively little circulation space in relation to the area of the rooms, and it permits the rooms to be narrow where there is no need for extra area and to widen out at the windows, although the awkward angles do create problems of their own.

Having discovered a design configuration that has certain advantages, Portman will reuse it wherever he finds it appropriate; but he learns from experience and makes improvements as he goes along. The cylindrical Peachtree Plaza Hotel and its Los Angeles and Detroit counterparts reflect a change in Portman's definition of what he calls public and private space. Instead of arranging the private spaces around a huge central public space, Portman more and more frequently is making the distinction horizontally: the lower floors are public, the upper floors private.

The Fort Worth bank building originally had a central space for its full height. As built, the office space is more or less conventional, with the elevators in a central core and all the spatial interest at the base of the tower (see section, plans, and photograph, pages 120–123).

Putting the elevators into the central core of the bank tower meant that it was no longer possible for the ride up to be a dramatic spatial experience. In the Peachtree Plaza Hotel, the elevators leading to the hotel rooms are in the core, but there are glass-walled cabs in an exterior structure for the ride to the rooftop restaurant. In the Los Angeles hotel there are more of these exterior elevators, and for the Renaissance Center in Detroit Portman was able to design an octagonal office building in which all the elevators will have a spectacular view of Detroit or the waterfront as they run up the exterior of the towers.

One building type for which Portman continues to find a large central space appropriate is the merchandise mart. There is one in the Merchandise Mart at Brussels, which Portman designed and developed in partnership with Trammell Crow. The Apparel Mart at Peachtree Center, now under construction, and the projected mart at Porte d'Ivry near Paris also have a central atrium, which gives unity and a sense of place to what would otherwise be an enormous windowless warehouse.

Comparing the Atlanta Apparel Mart with Portman's initial Merchandise Mart shows that Portman has come a long way as a designer from the first mart to the latest. The original mart is a straightforward and useful structure, but except for an arcade, a pool in the lobby, and a rooftop restaurant, it is simply a large box. The new structure incorporates a grandeur of spatial experience that was once thought to be possible only in important public buildings. One of Portman's achievements is to make such spaces part of everyday life.

While Portman was designing and developing Peachtree Center, he began work on two other large downtown building complexes: the Embarcadero Center in San Francisco and the Renaissance Center in Detroit. They show an evolution toward more and more integration of separate buildings into a single interdependent grouping, or coordinate downtown unit.

This view from Nob Hill in San Francisco, looking toward the bay, shows how Portman's office towers at Embarcadero Center, with their narrow offset slabs, minimize their bulk in comparison with the blocky silhouettes of most of the other office structures. The tower that resembles an oil derrick is the Transamerica Building.

The Embarcadero Center is part of an urban renewal project in an area of old warehouses adjoining the downtown business district of San Francisco. The land was assembled by the city and the existing buildings removed, so that there were none of the problems of obtaining land that produced the improvisatory growth of Peachtree Center. The successful bid for some of the land was tendered by a consortium of investors: Portman, Trammell Crow, and David Rockefeller, with Portman as the architect for the buildings and managing partner for the development.

Important aspects of the urban renewal project had already been completed, however, before Portman and his associates were brought in by the renewal authorities. These existing buildings rested on three

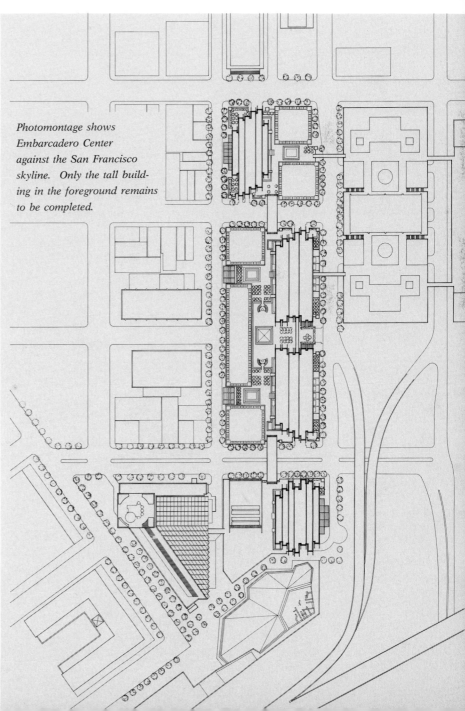

Photomontage shows Embarcadero Center against the San Francisco skyline. Only the tall building in the foreground remains to be completed.

The esplanade level at Embarcadero Center: top, looking east toward the bay, with the hotel at the extreme right; center, looking west toward the rest of downtown San Francisco. Below, the Sacramento Street side of the Embarcadero complex. Unlike other buildings in the Golden Gateway urban renewal plan, the Portman buildings are open and accessible from the street. Parking is below grade instead of occupying the stories between street and esplanade, as it does in neighboring structures.

stories of parking that formed a podium for the buildings, with the public spaces at the third-story plaza level.

Portman disagreed with this design concept, observing that it left the street-level sidewalk to run along for blocks against the dead walls of the parking garage. The Portman buildings have their garages in the basement and are designed to lead the pedestrian from the street, into the buildings, and up through them to a plaza level connected by bridges to the plaza already built. These public areas become an intricate multilevel combination of shops, escalators, and interpenetrating spaces instead of blank garage walls and an isolated plaza level.

Portman's design for the Embarcadero Center consists of a multilevel circulation "spine" connecting four office buildings, shopping, and a hotel, with the enormous interior court of the hotel playing an anchor role analogous to that of a department store in a shopping center. Site conditions imposed a great many design restraints. The need to preserve view corridors from Nob Hill and other locations caused Portman to offset the placement of the office towers and break up their bulk. The triangular block created by the intersection of Sacramento Street with the end of Market Street near the Ferry Terminal imposed a triangular form on the hotel.

The hotel was a requirement of the city's urban renewal plan. San Francisco is a city with many elegant places to stay, many of them far more interesting than the Embarcadero, which adjoins San Francisco's financial district. There is no other hotel for blocks in any direction. While this area has a certain built-in convenience for visiting businessmen, a routine building would have heavy competition from hotels on Nob Hill or around Union Square.

In designing this hotel, Portman again demonstrated that a spectacular urban space can have a strong positive effect on real estate marketability. The internal court, something like a triangular pyramid with two straight sides, was thronged with visitors before the rooms opened, and it continues to draw sightseers and customers for the hotel's bars and restaurants. Despite its out-of-the-way location, the occupancy rate is among the highest in San Francisco, with an average room rate at the top of the market.

The relationship of the large internal court to the office space will not be felt until all four office buildings have been completed and it is possible to enter the atrium from the bridge that connects it to the office tower on the north. You will enter on an axis with the spherical sculpture by Charles Perry that stands above a rectangular reflecting pool. From a low entranceway you will suddenly find yourself in the main space, with, as you look up to your right, the glass elevators that have become a Portman trademark shooting up to the apex of the seventeen-story room. At present, the space is revealed more gradually as you ride up the escalator from the lower floors.

As in Atlanta, galleries encircle the space at every level, but on the third side, the hypotenuse, each gallery leans a little farther out than the next, reflecting the hotel's terraced exterior. Full-size trees grow in rows, there are terraces and sidewalk cafés, and large crowds of people are all about you.

The hotel lobby, with its cafés and restaurants, is a meeting place for the whole Embarcadero Center.

47

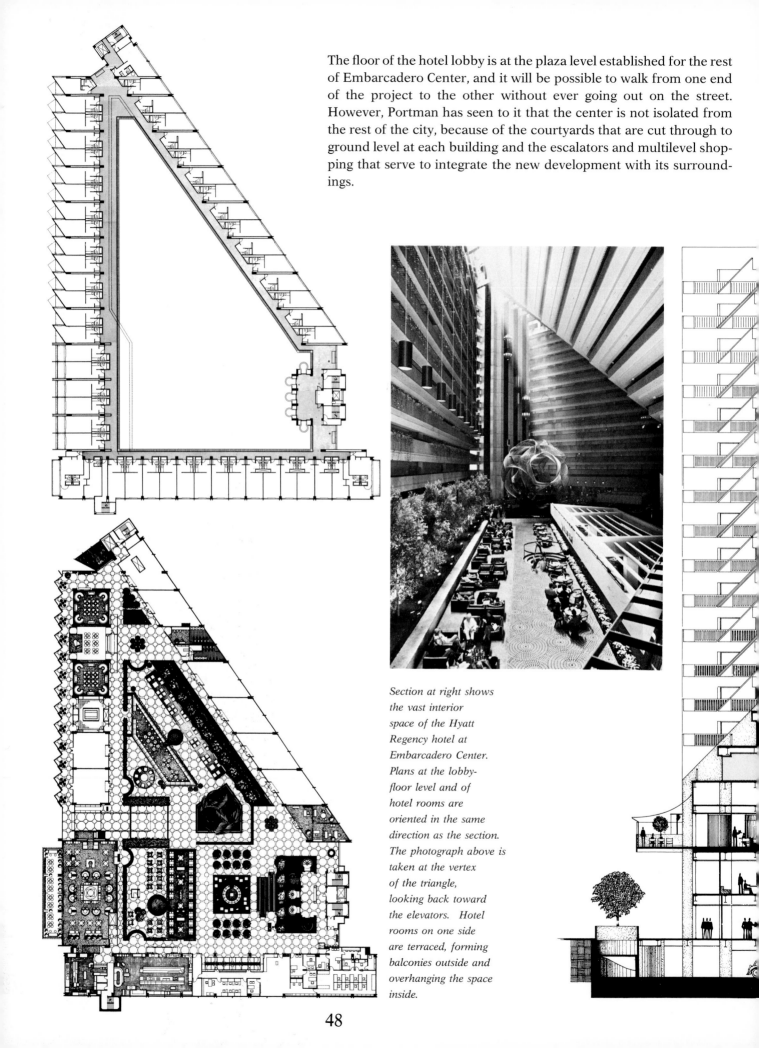

The floor of the hotel lobby is at the plaza level established for the rest of Embarcadero Center, and it will be possible to walk from one end of the project to the other without ever going out on the street. However, Portman has seen to it that the center is not isolated from the rest of the city, because of the courtyards that are cut through to ground level at each building and the escalators and multilevel shopping that serve to integrate the new development with its surroundings.

Section at right shows the vast interior space of the Hyatt Regency hotel at Embarcadero Center. Plans at the lobby-floor level and of hotel rooms are oriented in the same direction as the section. The photograph above is taken at the vertex of the triangle, looking back toward the elevators. Hotel rooms on one side are terraced, forming balconies outside and overhanging the space inside.

48

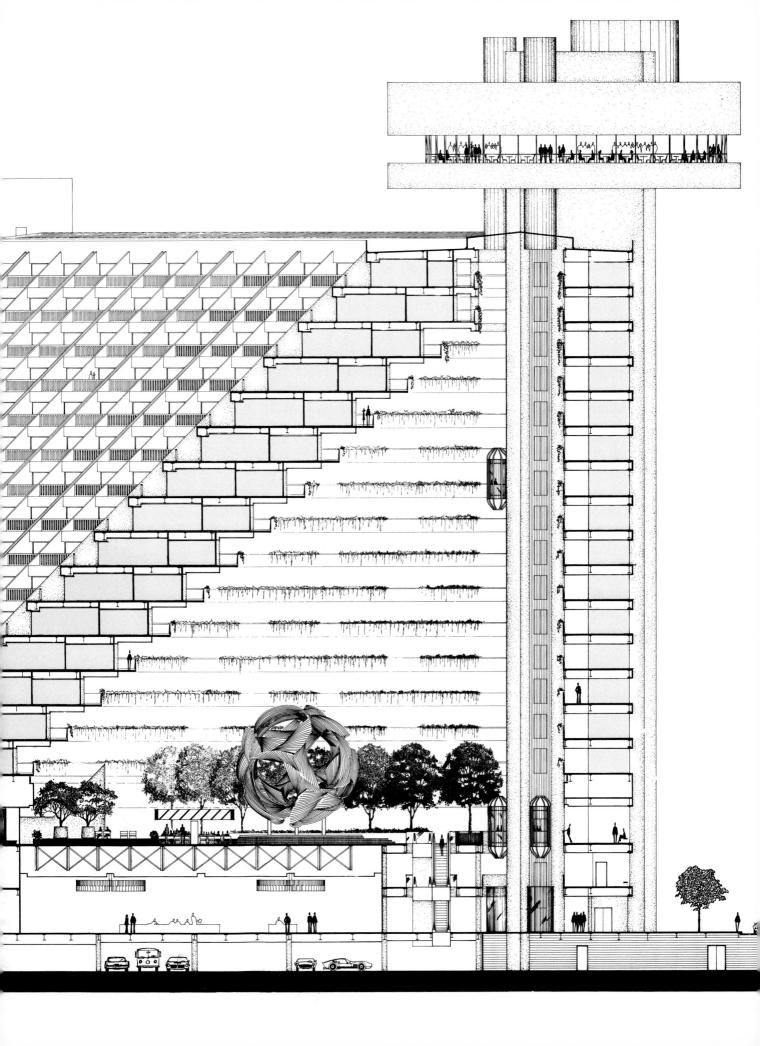

The Renaissance Center in Detroit is much more isolated. Financed by a consortium of Detroit businessmen and national corporations, with Henry Ford as the moving spirit, the center is intended to do what its name says: bring about the rebirth of downtown Detroit. It occupies 32 acres of cleared land along the waterfront; not only were there few existing buildings, but no streets need be kept open. The site was presented to Portman as an almost completely blank slate.

Portman's response was to make the connections between buildings the basis of the design. Detroit has a much harsher climate than either Atlanta or San Francisco; so Portman used his freedom from street grids and property lines to create a multilevel enclosed space that is an extremely high-powered version of the enclosed mall found in some of the more sophisticated suburban shopping centers. It is a world of its own, with lakes, shops, restaurants, and trees. The buildings are above, but in these public spaces you are aware only of the elevators, and if you know something about structural engineering, you may recognize the groups of columns that support the hotels, office buildings, and apartments. Critics can argue that the development is not so much a renaissance as a Noah's Ark. Since Renaissance Center is accessible by freeway from the suburbs, visitors can drive into it without going through downtown Detroit at all. Portman would reply that you have to start somewhere. He sees connections from the center growing back to meet and intertwine with the rest of downtown Detroit. He does not accept the criticism that the center is meant to replace the existing downtown. "Why build downtown at all in that case?" he asks. Portman also points out that the sponsors of the project have an unusually big equity investment and have accepted a relatively high level of risk in order to start with a large-enough development to make a difference in the future of the central city.

As architecture, Portman has created something that is beyond the individual building. The architectural model looks unusual; the buildings seem closer together than is normal, although actually they are separated by more than the width of the usual city street. But these are not individual buildings; they are units of something else that is part shopping center, part hotel, part office and apartments, growing into one another to form a coordinated building block for a whole city.

The Renaissance Center is an outside commission that came to John Portman as an architect and was not created by John Portman the

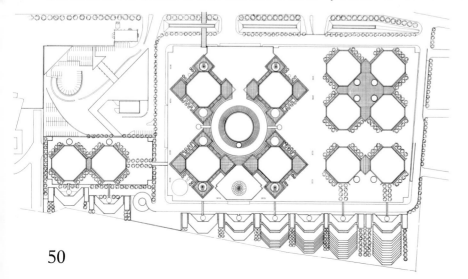

The Renaissance Center on the waterfront in Detroit is the most nearly complete example to date of Portman's coordinate unit. A hotel, offices, apartments, shops, and parking are combined in the 32-acre complex. The central section is under construction; the montage at left gives an impression of the way Detroit's skyline will look at night when all buildings are complete.

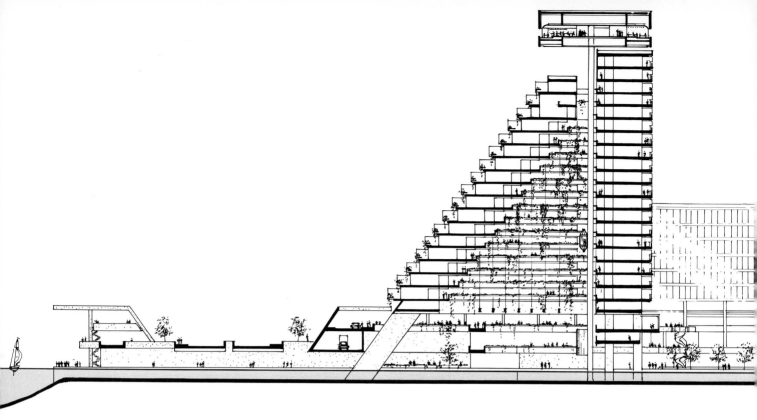

investor. It is, of course, unlikely that he would have received the commission or known what to do with it without his investment knowledge. Portman likes the discipline given by the requirements of an outside commission, the challenge of playing in a game where he hasn't also made up the rules, but his whole approach to design is conditioned by his understanding of the development context.

Wherever Portman works, he seems to bring the lessons back to Peachtree Center. The subway line that the Metropolitan Atlanta Rapid Transit Authority (MARTA) is building under Peachtree Street has given Portman an opportunity to work with the city, knitting together Peachtree Center, which has always been split by Peachtree Street, to make it more nearly unified, more of a coordinate unit. The

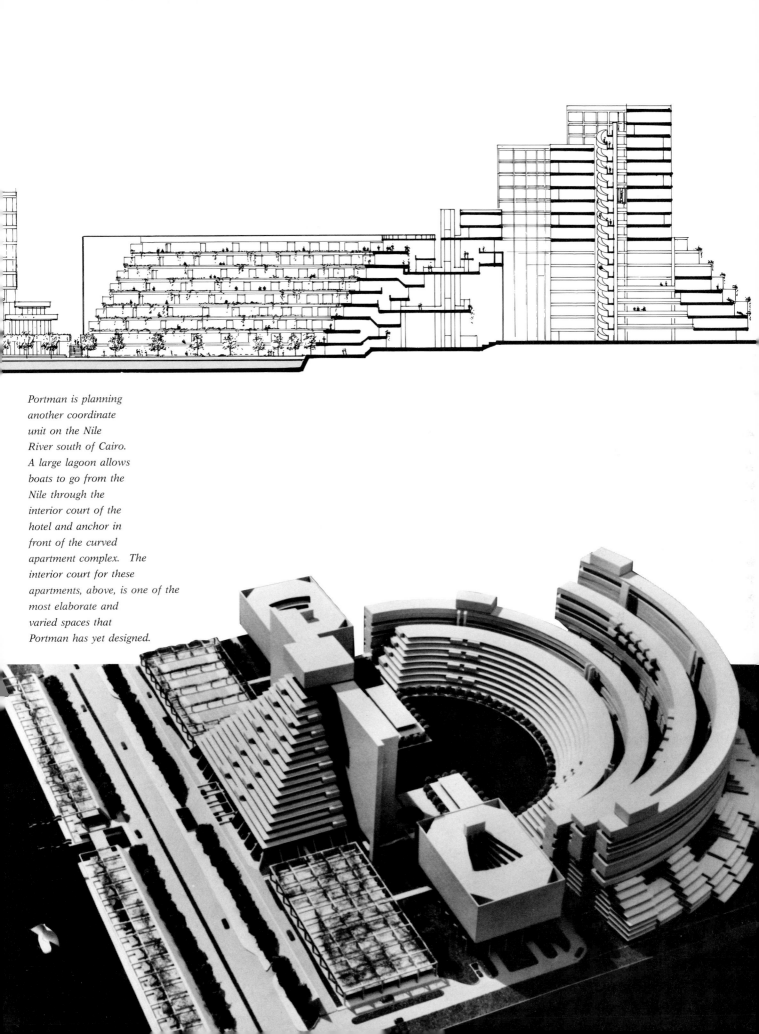

Portman is planning another coordinate unit on the Nile River south of Cairo. A large lagoon allows boats to go from the Nile through the interior court of the hotel and anchor in front of the curved apartment complex. The interior court for these apartments, above, is one of the most elaborate and varied spaces that Portman has yet designed.

subway station will connect directly into an underground concourse level that will serve all the buildings of the center. Portman had originally hoped that the topography, with Peachtree Street on the crest of a ridge, would permit a grade separation of traffic, to be accomplished at the time that the subway was excavated, with cross streets going under Peachtree and Peachtree itself becoming a mall, but this really major change is not part of MARTA's plans.

Portman's experience to date has caused him to feel that it is practical for the architect to operate on a large scale. He sees the architect as able to work for major change within the constraints of the existing social and financial system. His interest in urban centers has put him on the frontier of the urban crisis, the battle to preserve and improve our cities.

Portman's work puts him on the frontier of another important issue as well. At a time when architectural exhibitions and polemical articles are questioning the assumptions of modern architecture, Portman is able to show the results of fifteen years of work, during which he has been seeking to reformulate his approach to design in order to make his buildings more responsive to the human spirit and the needs of everyday life.

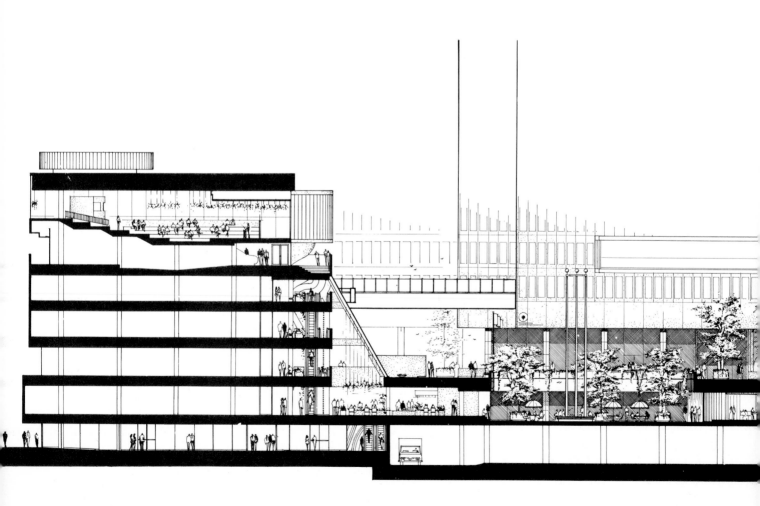

Transverse section through Peachtree Center shows the relationship of the new rapid transit station to the many levels of the center itself. The photograph is taken looking toward Peachtree Street.

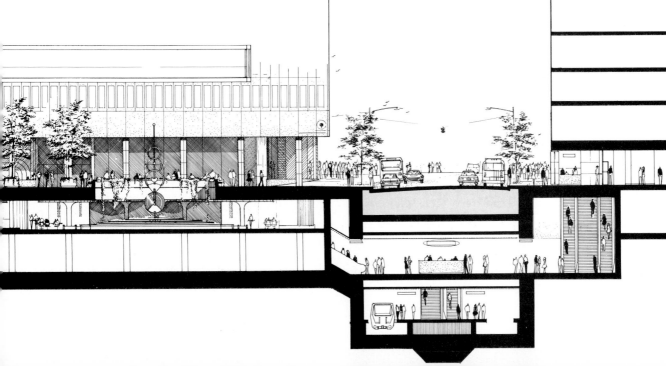

Part 2: Architecture

as a social art

An architecture
for people
and not
for things

by John Portman

"Things are in the saddle,
And ride mankind." Ralph Waldo Emerson

It is time for a new definition of architecture and of the architect's role in society. For many years the profession gained its sense of purpose and direction by creating an architecture that would incorporate and express the technology of our time. That battle for modern architecture has now been won. The important issue today is the design of the environment. Architects must redirect their energies toward an environmental architecture, born of human needs and responding to vital physical, social, and economic circumstances. They must work at a larger scale and with more complex problems than they have in the past, but they must not give up the ultimate goal of transmuting their material into works of art.

Architects should not be intimidated by the idea of designing at a large scale. No matter how large a project is, you can find the most appropriate solution, if the essence of the problem can be isolated and understood.

When architects begin to study a new situation, they confront a mass of irrelevancy and confusion. They must work their way through to that kernel of truth that defines the problem in a clear and concise way. Then they can start spinning outward from this definition, evolving a solution that has an appropriateness derived from the unique qualities of the problem at hand. It then becomes their job to preserve the integrity of this conception throughout the evolution of the project, to the day of its completion.

Frank Lloyd Wright was describing such a process when he wrote about "organic" architecture. Louis Kahn said much the same thing when he spoke of a building "wanting to be"; so did Eero Saarinen when he talked about a search for the "spirit" of the building.

I don't know what visual form a building or a group of buildings will take until it comes clear through this conceptual process. It is often a temptation to start with an image, or some other preconceived idea, and then manipulate the actual situation until it meets the preconception. Down this road lies mediocrity at best. I seek to open all windows of the mind, taking nothing for granted. I follow Emerson in saying that in the light of new knowledge I will take a new position, even if it conflicts with what I have said or done in the past.

Perhaps it seems a contradiction that you can find design ideas in one or another of my buildings similar to designs I have developed and used elsewhere. Often, the reason for such similarities is that the same kinds of problems are involved. In addition, while I am attempting to develop an appropriate solution to each essential problem, I am also seeking to build up a consistent design philosophy.

Architects must have such a philosophy if they are to prevent a dissipation of their energies. A design philosophy is the rudder for the boat; it makes possible a continuing course in a meaningful direction.

I first began thinking seriously about such guiding principles of architecture and design when I made a trip to South America for the dedication ceremonies at Brasília in 1960. I was very excited about the prospect of seeing a new city completely designed by architects, but it was not long before the excitement of anticipation turned to disappointment. What an inhuman place! Nothing but great blocks of buildings arranged in military order. Some of the architecture is actually quite interesting, but the buildings seen together become objects arranged in a sterile, two-dimensional pattern that shows no understanding of human scale or of the need for people to become involved in their surroundings. I found that after one look there was no desire to walk down the street, turn the corner, and suddenly discover something, because I already knew what was there.

This trip to Brasília made me realize that many of the design concepts that had come to be accepted by the architectural profession did not work very well at the scale of an entire city. Older cities, no matter how badly their designs had evolved, were still better at providing for human needs than Brasília, whatever the virtues of the architecture. I came to the conclusion that what we needed to do in the United States was to restructure our existing cities, not build new ones.

I returned to Atlanta resolved to improve my abilities as an architect in two ways: first, to learn how to design at the scale of the city; and, second, to find ways of making buildings more responsive to human values.

We had just finished the largest building in Atlanta, the Merchandise Mart, at one of the major intersections, and I felt that we could not allow just anything to happen up and down the block and across the street. Why not take the first steps toward creating a larger-scale environment? So we started assembling land. We gained control of the plots next door to the mart and parcels in other key locations, with the specific aim of creating a new environment that followed a master development plan, would grow step by step, and would add to, not obliterate, the life, vitality, and interest of the existing city.

At this time I had an opportunity to design a house for my growing family; and I concluded that if an architect is ever going to face himself and probe the essence of architecture, there is no better place to start than his own house. There is no excuse other than monetary that one can use. I felt the need to develop a design philosophy in which I could believe, one that would give direction and force to my architecture.

It was over the design of this house that I started to ponder seriously the various ingredients of architecture, including space, order, a need for variety, structure, light, color, and materials. I also realized that I must try to understand human reactions and responses to environmental space.

Architecture is not a private affair; even a house must serve a whole family and its friends, and most buildings are used by everybody, people from all walks of life. If a building is to meet the needs of all the people, the architect must look for some common ground of understanding and experience.

The need for this common ground led me back to people as creatures of nature, perceiving their environment through the five senses. I decided that if I learned to weave elements of sensory appeal into the design, I would be reaching those innate responses that govern how a human being reacts to the environment. In that way I could create environments that all people would instinctively find harmonious.

I came to call these principles that derive from people's relation to their environment "constants." Architects spend most of their time learning to deal with variables: the immediate physical constraints, site conditions, what's happening in and around the building, what the structure has to do under a particular set of circumstances—circumstances that might not exist in another situation.

The definition of the design problem comes from understanding the essence of the variables, but the solution evolves through the application of constants, principles of design that hold true in every case. The resulting design should be a marriage of the constants and the variables.

Floor plans of Portman house in Atlanta. Guests enter at upper level and look down into two-story living room and study to their left. A pool runs through the house at the lower level; the dining table is on a circular island. The house can become a single large pavilion for a party or be divided into separate units for privacy.

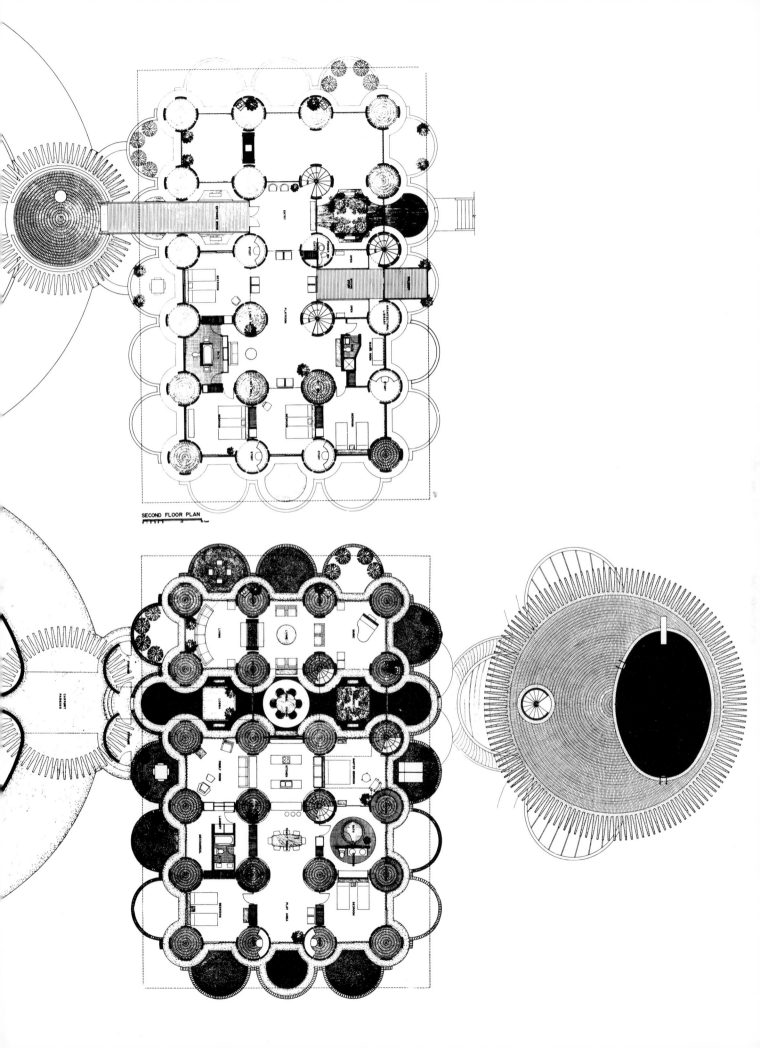

SECOND FLOOR PLAN

Another way to understand this opposition of principles and practical obstacles is to speak of statics and dynamics.

Architects in the past have tended to concentrate their attention on the building as a static object.   I believe dynamics are more important: the dynamics of people, their interaction with spaces and environmental conditions.   Architects must learn to understand humanity better so that they can create an environment that is more beneficial to people, more rewarding, more pleasant to experience.   I'm naturally interested in the latest structural techniques, in innovative building materials and the technology of my craft; but I am more interested in people.   Buildings should serve people, not the other way around.

If you go back and analyze the history of architecture, most buildings that historians consider important are objects built to the greater glory of God, or an individual, or a political system; they are not environments for people to live in.   One purpose of the pyramids was to express political domination: the little man can't look up without seeing the tomb of his king.   The cathedrals dominated the towns in which they were built.   The great Haussmann plan for nineteenth-century Paris, which has given such pleasure to so many people, was carried out partly to assist Napoleon III in keeping control of the city: great boulevards, wonderful trees, but the motive of domination is also there.

Most office buildings are built to serve only narrow corporate objectives. They are saying: "I'm Mr. Big: look how powerful I am, what strength I have, what security."

When you analyze the buildings you see every day and the motives behind them, you find that most are not created with any comprehensive view of what people need.   What I wanted to do as an architect was to create buildings and environments that really are for people, not a particular class of people but all people.

It was in my house that I first began to experiment with the concepts that I had identified as constant elements in the way that people relate to their environment.   Perhaps I am the only one who can see it, but much of my later work is implicit in that house.   It contains the basis for my architectural philosophy: organizing principles that work for a room or a restaurant, a building or a group of buildings.

Order
and
variety
simultaneously
achieved

In drama, the play is the thing; the stage, the scenery, and the lighting are important, but they serve a subordinate purpose. In architecture, space is the thing, and architects must be careful not to overemphasize elements that should be subordinate to space, such as structure, materials, light, or color. But space has no existence except as it is defined, and order is a necessary element of spatial definition. Innately, human beings, because they are capable of reason, require an order to things. Order creates a sense of comfort and well-being. But the mind craves variety at the same time that it requires order. At Brasília, too much order becomes something the mind abhors. What is needed is an order strong enough to permit variety and informality without losing the integrity that creates a harmonious environment: order and variety simultaneously achieved.

The 8-foot hollow columns in my house created a strong structural order, almost classical in nature, yet left me free to place a variety of different functions and experiences in just two basic kinds of space.

Each column is made up of eight separate panels. The ones on the four main axes are structural; the other four can be omitted to meet different conditions. A house is one of the very few building types that lends itself to the concepts of major and minor spaces as Louis Kahn defined them. The 8-foot diameter of the columns is a dimension large enough to contain the minor functions of the house and to integrate structure, space, light, and ventilation. These hollow columns function as stairways, hallways,

The Midnight Sun restaurant in Peachtree Center. A strongly geometric design can still create many small spaces, which provide privacy and a diversity of experiences.

66

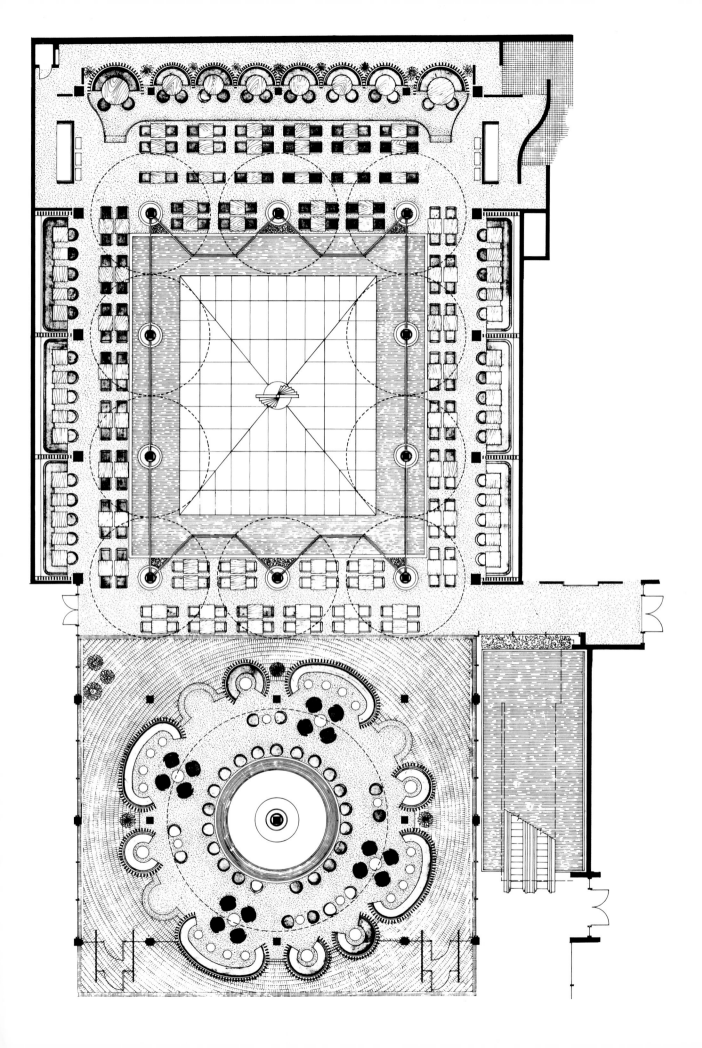

children's study rooms, a library, a powder room, and small galleries for sculpture. They leave the larger areas free so that there is a flow of related spaces from one end of the house to the other. When all the doors are open, the house becomes a pavilion; when the doors are closed, we have clearly defined areas for individual privacy, for children, for adults, and for entertaining.

The wooden, treelike columns at the Midnight Sun restaurant in Peachtree Center are used to define a strong, orderly system of spatial organization. They even extend beyond the glass line into the courtyard to help integrate indoors and outdoors. At the same time, there is a system of niches and pockets of space that give individual tables their own private environment. You are aware of your intimate immediate surroundings and the whole restaurant, simultaneously. Space is allowed to flow in such a way that you can see from the cocktail lounge in the front all the way to the opposite end of the restaurant; yet you are always in your own intimate area. This duality is achieved by space modulation.

The floor plans of the hotels I designed for Chicago and Los Angeles can be compared, not for their superficial resemblances, which are misleading, but for their systems of order. In a large and complex structure, it is important that you always know where you are in relation to the whole. One can achieve this systematic organization and still leave room for the variety of activities that every hotel must accommodate.

Wooden "trees" and hanging "vines" of geometric wooden blocks help define the spaces of the Midnight Sun restaurant at Peachtree Center, as does the contrast between carpet and brick flooring.

69

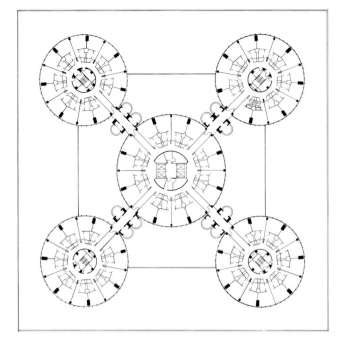

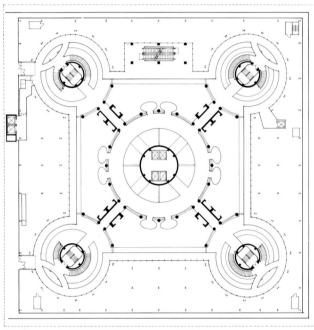

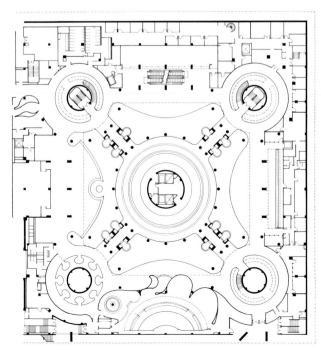

Right:
The floor plan of the
Hyatt Regency O'Hare
hotel, near the airport
in Chicago, shows that
the design follows a
simple, orderly pattern.
The main space, with
bridges alternating
their direction at each
floor, is highly complex,
however, and
suggests some of the
architectural fantasies
of Piranesi.

Left:
Three levels of the
Bonaventure Hotel in
Los Angeles. Top, a
typical floor, which
provides a very compact
and efficient arrangement.

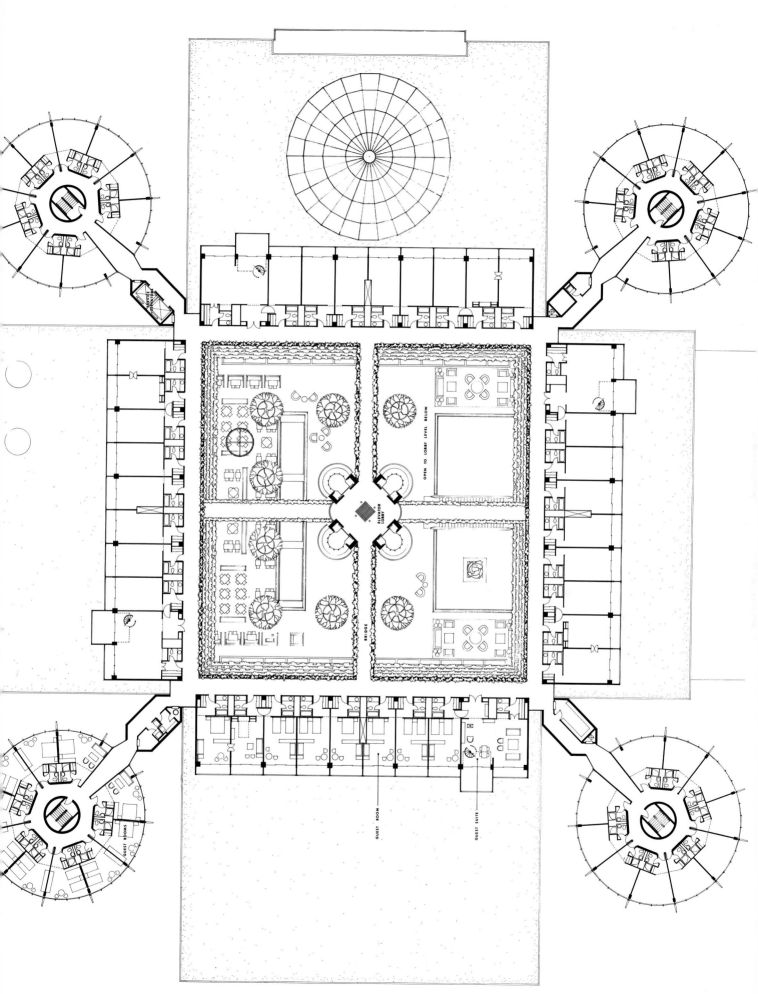

GUEST ROOM

GUEST SUITE

GUEST ROOMS

OPEN TO LOBBY LEVEL BELOW

ELEVATOR LOBBY

BRIDGE

SERVICE ELEVATOR

71

Movement

Different architectural spaces create different emotional responses. When people move through a building, their journey should be orchestrated. Architects should articulate the journey into a sequence of spaces, ranging from tight enclosures to large volumes. They should understand how different spatial volumes relate to the individual, not only in a static but also in a dynamic way. There should also be places that produce a neutral emotional effect, in the same way that a piece of bread cleanses the palate between two wines. What I call "people scoops" are designed to be such places of transition, from outdoors to indoors or from one kind of space to another.

Riding an escalator is also a transitional experience, and it can be used in such a way that the space you are entering is gradually revealed. That is why, in the hotel in San Francisco, I had the escalators bring people up facing away from the main space. I wanted a more gradual realization than you get in the Regency hotel in Atlanta, where you walk through a low entranceway, a people scoop, directly into the central atrium. When you enter on an escalator, I want the space to unfold rather than explode upon you all at once.

Riding in an elevator is another important transitional experience, and there is no reason why you must ride in a closed-in box. Pulling the elevator out of its shaft and opening it up with walls of glass makes it another way of experiencing architectural space. The elevator is like a seat in a theater, but

Portman believes that entering a building on an escalator should produce a gradually increasing awareness of the space. At right, the entrance to the Hyatt Regency O'Hare hotel.

one in which your vantage point is moving continuously. When people step into an ordinary elevator, all conversation tends to stop; when people ride in a glass-enclosed elevator they are much more likely to go on talking. That happens because they are taking part in an interesting and humane experience; they are not isolated and shut away.

Movement is also interesting to watch. Movement in people, objects, and water, and even the sounds of movement are important. I've never met anyone who didn't like a log fire. After all, society started around a log fire. There seems to be some innate reaction between human beings and fire in a social context. People are fascinated by kinetics. One of the attractions of the log fire is the dancing flames. They are almost hypnotic. People are innately interested in movement, for movement means life, and human beings are kinetic creatures. You can incorporate kinetics in a building and strike a responsive human reaction.

When you are having lunch in the café at the Shopping Gallery in Peachtree Center, you can watch people moving up and down the escalators. You can also watch the moving lights above the escalators, which show the direction in which the escalators are going. At the cafés in the hotels I have designed there are places where you can watch the movement of the elevator cabs, which become a huge kinetic sculpture. There is an element of unpredictability; you are never sure which cab will move next or in what direction.

Escalator in the Shopping Gallery at Peachtree Center is also placed so that the space you are entering gradually unfolds before you. Below, moving lights in the Shopping Gallery symbolize movement and direction of escalator.

*The elevator as a way
of experiencing
architectural space.*

Curving stairs at
Embarcadero Center.
Below, right, Portman
on the stair at his office
in Atlanta.

81

"People scoops" at left create a transitional space between indoors and outdoors: above, Embarcadero Center; below, the Blue Cross building in Chattanooga. Bridges are also a transitional space.

Light, color, and materials

Modern architecture, as practiced at the Bauhaus and defined by the phrase "International Style," started out being very machinelike, very cold. Many people still find that this kind of building is hard to live with over a long period of time. I think that architects were so anxious to design for our modern technological age that they forgot how important light, color, texture, and materials are in humanizing a building, creating warmth, making it livable. Le Corbusier, who once said that a house was a machine for living and who worked with slick stucco finishes, glass, and white paint, had obviously changed his ideas about design by the end of his life. His later buildings were reaching for something the machine left out: the sense of the human hand, the feel of rough concrete and boards, the awareness that things can age and change with age.

Le Corbusier's early, machinelike buildings still have a strong influence. They, along with the buildings of Mies van der Rohe and others, have helped to make architecture very puritanical; architects today are still hesitant about how they use light, color, and materials to create warmth.

Light—both natural and artificial light—is one of the least understood and one of the most important elements in the design of any building. The ambient light in a space can change the whole personality of an environment. The play of natural light is always moving and changing because of the weather or the time of day or year. The architect must design with an understanding of the effects that different light quantities and qualities have on a space and the resulting effect on the human being.

Most structures are used both day and night, and artificial light becomes a necessity. Artificial light should grow out of and reinforce the structure of a space in its most idealized form. Light is what brings space to life, and it should reinforce the volume and awareness of the space. You should be aware of the quality of light in the space and not of the light itself, except where the light source is being used as a feature, such as a chandelier or other frankly decorative application. There are many examples one can observe. The swimming pool in the Chicago O'Hare Regency hotel that I designed for Hyatt is covered by a plastic dome. To modulate this space and soften what would otherwise be a very harsh environment, I hung four huge umbrellas of yellow fabric. By day they give shade and add color; at night they become glowing lanterns and create a festive atmosphere for cocktail parties around the pool.

I use color very sparingly and always deliberately as an integral part of an environmental entity. Sometimes it is used in a sculptural form that complements a space, as it is in the tubular sculpture of Japanese kites that I designed for the same Chicago hotel that has the domed swimming pool. I also use color as large-scale curvilinear graphics on banners and walls and sequences of fabric hangings to add softness to constructed space and to define important places.

A tubular sculpture of Japanese kites creates a counterpoint to the concrete structure of the Chicago hotel. At night the tube is illuminated from within.

A building wants to be all one thing in the end and, in its most idealized form, would be an entity created from a single material. The many factors involved in construction seldom permit such a solution, but it is important to remember that greater dignity and integrity lie in using the smallest number of different materials.

The structure and materials form space, and light reveals it; but both should be subordinate to it. Everything that has a role in the environment of a space must be orchestrated to produce its character and evoke a sense of well-being in the individual.

Umbrellas of
yellow fabric hang
from the plexiglass
dome above the swimming
pool in the Chicago hotel,
softening what would
otherwise be a very harsh
environment. At night
the umbrellas become
glowing lanterns.
At right, another kind
of yellow umbrella enlivens
the garden court at
Peachtree Center.

Trees and vines can create an unexpected oasis of privacy in the middle of a bustling city.

Most constructed environments are rectilinear because it is more economical to build them that way. But it is easier for a human being to feel affinity with curvilinear forms; they are more lifelike, more natural. Whether you are looking at the waves in the ocean, the rolling hills of land, or the billowing forms of clouds in the sky, there are no hard, straight lines.

As you fly over the earth and gaze below, you will see where people are by the lines on the ground. In pure nature unaltered by human beings, you will see no straight lines, but as you begin to approach civilization, you will begin to see the square, the rectangle, and the straight line in the landscape, the checkerboard pattern produced by human intellect. Human intellect relates to the straight line, but emotions are tied to the curvilinear forms of nature. Both represent needs that must be met to satisfy the human creature fully. If you draw a straight line, you will feel it in your head, but if you draw a flowing line, you will feel it in your heart.

People are prone to think in straight lines because they can objectify their intellect better than they can their emotions. Their innate emotions cause stirrings that they do not understand and somehow cannot explain. Artists listen to their hearts and produce works that are in concert with nature.

Why is the circle considered the purest of all forms? Is it because it relates to both intellect and emotions? It is a form that symbolizes the cyclical movements which are an embodiment of nature, and yet it is a clear and conscious form which people understand intellectually. It satisfies their rational and emotional needs.

For these reasons, I use curvilinear forms in my buildings in apposition to the rectilinear constructed environment. Colored fabrics, flowers, and landscaping are other means that can be used to soften the rigidity of architecture, making it easier for people to relate to a building.

Throughout nature there are subtle transitions in color, texture, and form. One rarely encounters abrupt or harsh contrasts in nature. There is an underlying harmony in the natural environment that is very appealing to the human being. There are endless clues in nature that can teach architects to equip the constructed environment for human habitation. Why does one feel a sense of freedom and tranquillity walking through a forest, sitting by a bubbling brook, or even looking out across a lake or an ocean? Human beings are a natural extension of all this and, at the same time, are indigenous to it. They have a natural affinity to beautiful landscapes, flowers, and foliage, to running water, fountains, and waterfalls. Such things are part of nature, and they are also part of human beings. They are constants.

Plants and trees can be used as an important way of forming space and modifying light in buildings. As the sun comes through foliage, it makes patterns. The light in the Shopping Gallery at Peachtree Center is filtered through hanging plants; it makes a pattern in the café like shadows on the floor of a forest. The plants also lower the ceiling, giving a sense of enclosure without blocking out a sense of the larger space.

Rows of trees can modify space, create and define separate areas. They can also provide places of solitude and privacy in the midst of the city's crowds and confusion.

I have at times put cages of birds into large spaces. They are another element of nature that gives life and movement. In the Embarcadero hotel in San Francisco, I have also introduced a "sound sculpture" by Bernhard Leitner that creates the impression of a flock of birds flying in, alighting on the trees, and bursting into song. I use elements of nature to make a connection between the built environment and the human psyche. They are human environmental connections.

Trees, flowers, birds, and a brook at the hotel in Embarcadero Center.

Nature is a connector between people and the constructed environment.

Water

Water can be used in architecture to evoke memories of the natural environment: a brook, a fountain, a waterfall, or a lake. People respond to water. They put their hands into a sheet of water to see what will happen; they watch reflections, movement. Water is kinetic, active; water also makes sounds, provides a background. It is one of the elements that can transform a building from a static object to a dynamic environment.

The sheet of water at the Embarcadero Center hotel presents an irresistible temptation.

Three ways to
use water:
at the Midnight
Sun restaurant,
above left; the
lake at the
Peachtree Center
hotel; and, at right,
a fountain at
Embarcadero Center.
(The building with the
exoskeleton at far right
is the Alcoa Building,
by Skidmore, Owings and
Merrill.)

*Artificial nature:
treelike columns rising
from the lake at Renaissance
Center; shimmering glass
beads for a chandelier
that create an effect
not unlike a waterfall;
hanging lucite geometric
shapes, part icicle and
part vine.*

People
watching
people

People enjoy watching a changing scene. This is very obvious. I learned from visiting the Tivoli Gardens in Copenhagen that one of its main attractions is the opportunity for people to watch other people. That is the attraction of the sidewalk café. Everybody who goes to Paris has to walk the Champs-Élysées, and here are all the sidewalk cafés. There is some magic about it, whether you are sitting in a café watching other people or walking up and down the sidewalk yourself. Some people enjoy watching other people more than they enjoy having other people watch them; others like to be on the stage, part of the passing parade.

We don't have a tradition of sitting in similar public places in the United States; everyone runs up and down the sidewalks like rats. But when Americans go to Europe, they gravitate to the sidewalk cafés. I don't believe in mimicking the historic European cities (or anything else for that matter), but I think we can create opportunities for the same kinds of experiences.

Shared
space

The whole concept of shared space is based on the human desire for a release from confinement. If more than one thing is happening in a space, if you can look out from one area and be conscious of other activities going on, it gives you a sense of spiritual freedom.

The first time I went into St. Peter's in Rome, the space made an emotional impact on me that I shall always remember. Here we are, living in an age of 8-foot, 6-inch ceilings and asphalt tile floors. We forget that architectural space can affect us emotionally. Of course, the kind of space created for a major cathedral by the genius of Michelangelo represents a very special situation. St. Peter's for me was not a model but a reminder of what a big space can do.

I also recall very vividly the first time I went into the Guggenheim Museum in New York. Frank Lloyd Wright designed this museum so that you go up to the top in an elevator and then walk down the ramp, which is a continuous curving gallery that opens out onto a big central space.

About halfway down the ramp, I began analyzing why this experience felt so good and worked so well. I would look at a few paintings, and then I'd walk over to the rail, look around and see people, look down into the space, and then go back and look at more paintings. I also observed that other people were doing the same thing. Anybody who goes through a museum and finds himself being led from one closed compartment to another knows that he soon longs for relief. In that respect the Guggenheim is very successful. You can go through it comfortably and leave without feeling fatigued or bored.

Architectural space can create continual interest and surprise.

The principle of design that makes the Guggenheim work so well is the concept of shared space.

When you design a space, that's not the end of it.   You have to articulate it for human involvement.   A ceiling at around 7 feet can create a strong sense of enclosure; as you raise the ceiling, this feeling of protection diminishes.   That is why I projected a trellis structure out from the balcony-corridors of the Regency hotel in Atlanta at a height of about 7 feet.   It gives you a sense of shelter as you look out, as well as softening the impact of looking directly down, because you see the lobby through the trellises below you.   You have the exhilaration of the big space, and you also have other, smaller spaces that are easy to use and feel comfortable.

If you sit in the café of the San Francisco Regency Hyatt hotel in Embarcadero Center, you are sitting under a low enclosure that gives a feeling of intimacy; and yet you look out on a large space and are exposed to another experience.   Other things are happening, but they don't impinge on you.

In the building I designed for the Fort Worth National Bank, sharing space creates a new approach to a bank building.   The actual banking floor is on a lower level, below the street.   When you enter from the street, you find that you are on a bridge that leads to the elevators for the office building and the escalators going down to the bank.   There is a circular balcony cantilevered from the central core hovering in the space above.   This floating balcony is a restaurant.   Therefore, these three separate functions— the banking room, the office building lobby, and the restaurant—exist in a single large space combining all the public areas of the building yet not impinging on each other.

Certain activities belong in private spaces, others to public space.   The distinction is important; typical office floors do not have many public functions.   The activities which do involve the public usually cannot justify the expense of a large space.   In a typical bank building, the banking room is in a separate pavilion, the elevator lobby is at the base of the office tower, and the restaurant occupies a separate space somewhere else, usually on top of the offices.   By pooling the public spaces, it was possible to create a much grander volume than each would occupy individually.   In addition, this is a space that says "bank."   No one enters or leaves the building without understanding the basic identity of the structure.

Section through bank headquarters building in Fort Worth. Banking floor is below grade, elevator lobby is reached by bridges, and there is a restaurant above. Each use enjoys a large space that could not be justified for any single function on its own.

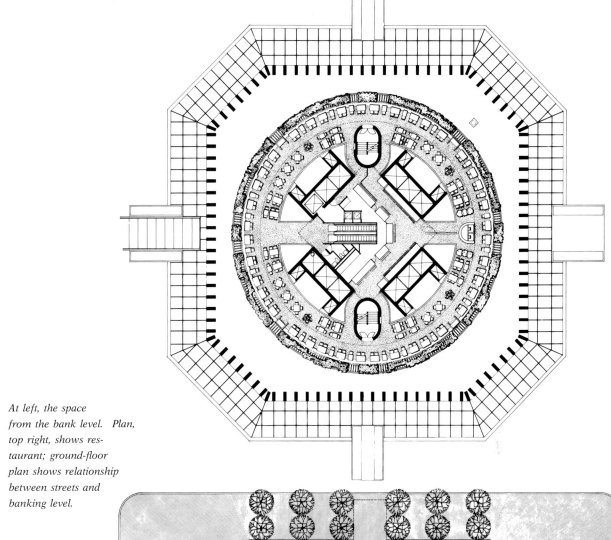

At left, the space from the bank level. Plan, top right, shows restaurant; ground-floor plan shows relationship between streets and banking level.

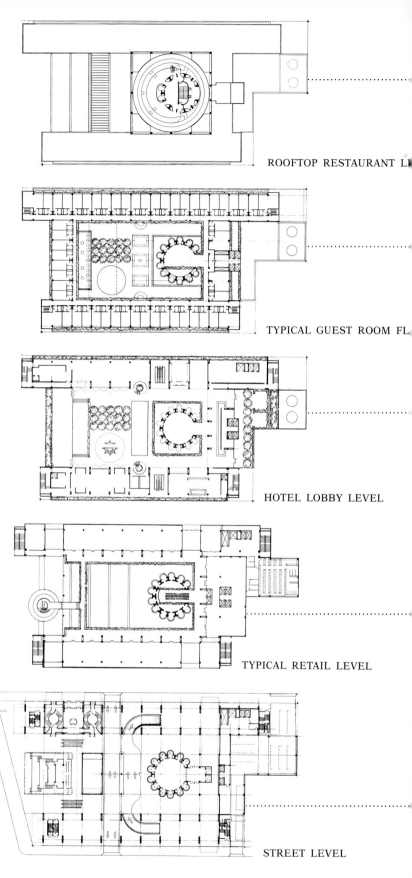

ROOFTOP RESTAURANT L[

TYPICAL GUEST ROOM FL[

HOTEL LOBBY LEVEL

The proposed Times Square hotel would have two major spaces: one for the seven levels of retail stores; a second, thirty-two stories high, for the hotel itself.

TYPICAL RETAIL LEVEL

STREET LEVEL

124

PARKING AND THEATER LEV[

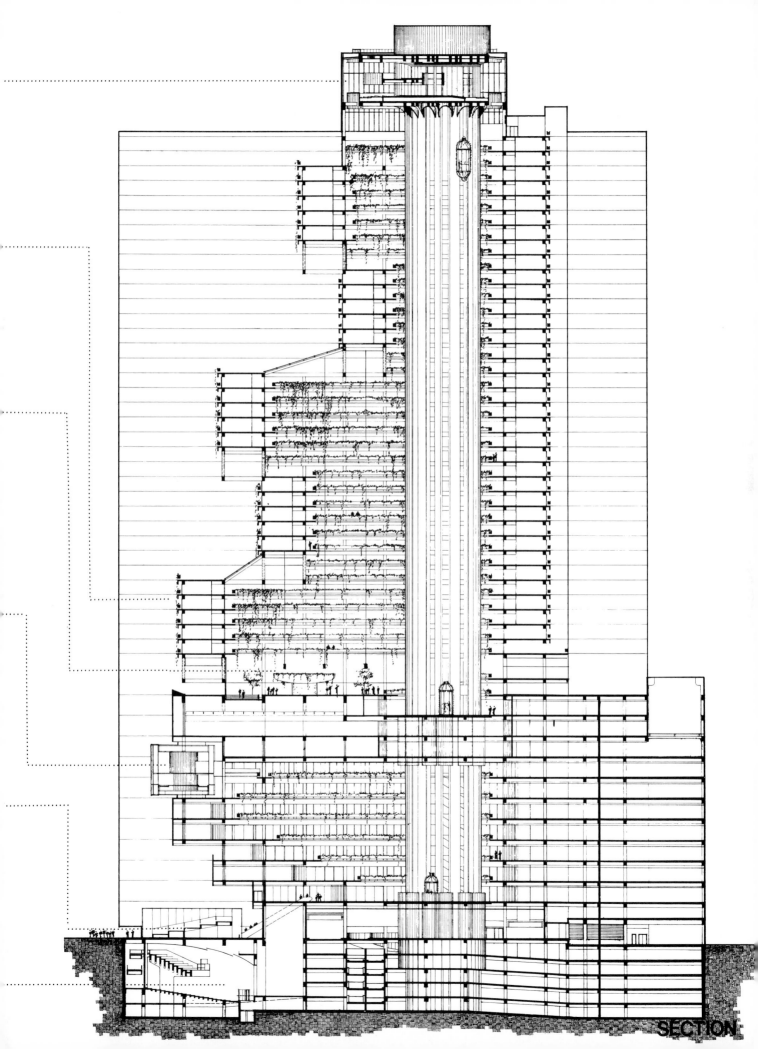

SECTION

*Main space of the
projected Merchandise
Mart at Porte d'Ivry,
near Paris,
provides an organizing
concept for
a huge
warehouse-like
building.*

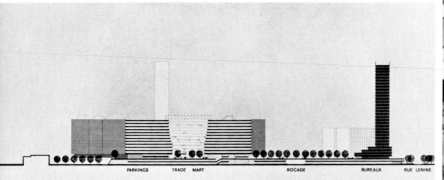

PARKINGS   TRADE MART   ROCADE   BUREAUX   RUE LENINE

The coordinate unit

Model photo of the first stage of Renaissance Center shows how five buildings become a single intricate organism.

We cannot afford to abandon the cities; it is a course of action that makes no sense either economically, politically, or socially. And if we do not intend to abandon our cities, we must stop acting as if that is what we are going to do. We must learn to restructure cities, to make them economically healthy and desirable places for people to live and work in.

A city is not a fixed object like an individual building. A city is a living entity that is changing all the time. You do not design a city in the way that you design a building; but you can make a city a humane environment, not just in isolated places but continuously, throughout its whole fabric.

My ideas about cities began to expand and change in the mid-1960s, when I made my first journey to Scandinavia. The Tivoli Gardens in Copenhagen were a revelation to me. It is, perhaps, the most appealing place that I have seen, the one which people seem to enjoy most. I am sure that this quality is in part a reflection of the Danish people, whom I have found to be unfailingly warm and friendly and who have a great zest for life. When you walk through Tivoli, you see that almost everyone is smiling. I have given much thought to just which ingredients create the magic of the place. It has taught me much about the effect that environment can have on one's feelings.

From Copenhagen I went to Stockholm, where I saw two of the new satellite cities, Vällingby and Farsta. I was struck by something I saw on my way into Vällingby. There is a highway running along the edge of the city center and a pedestrian bridge that goes across it. I saw a woman pushing a baby carriage over this bridge and realized that she was going from her apartment to the town center to do her shopping. Then I noticed that most of the apartment buildings were placed so that you could come right down into the central city through the green areas. I began to see that this is really what it is all about: people walking over from their houses to do their shopping, and their kids coming over, and the freedom of that kind of environment separated from the wheels of the motor car. The highway was there, and rapid transit was available, but you didn't need to use a car every time you had to do a simple errand.

I was not impressed with the buildings, and I did not feel that the city center was executed well from a design point of view; but there was a germ of an idea there, something quite different from the sterile modernism of a place like Brasília.

130

This trip also included a visit to Helsinki, where I was greatly impressed by the excellence of the architecture for the satellite community of Tapiola, although I felt that it was too dependent on the automobile. The Tapiola plan is still the old campus plan related to wheels.

The overall experience gained from Tivoli, Vällingby, and Tapiola led me to realize that the way you should go about designing and evolving an environment is by thinking about what people want and need on a day-to-day basis. Perhaps this may not seem a very surprising idea, but it has never been done on a large scale. You can walk up and down Park Avenue in New York and see buildings that hold huge numbers of people, but what thought has been given to these people or to the kind of life that the buildings create? Not very much. Every city is the result of a great many individual decisions, most of them made by government and businesses for their own institutional or corporate reasons. It is incredible how little is done for the good of ordinary people. Every city has to go back and say: "OK, this whole thing is for that little guy who is walking around down there. How can we have this huge mass of density, and profit, and all the rest of it and still create a livable environment?"

I have come to the conclusion that cities ought to be designed in a cellular pattern whose scale is the distance that an individual will walk before he thinks of wheels. What information and observations we have available on this question indicate that the average American is willing to walk from seven to ten minutes without looking for some form of transportation. Using this time-distance factor as a radius gives a surprisingly large area.

If this area is developed into a total environment in which practically all of a person's needs are met, you have what I call a coordinate unit, a village where everything is within reach of the pedestrian. You could walk to work, school, church, recreation, shopping, entertainment, and so on without having to get into a car or any other kind of transit unless you were going outside the cellular unit. What great savings in energy and time, what great convenience such a city design could produce!

Peachtree Center is the beginning of such an urban coordinate unit. We are now building the commercial core and plan to add housing and the other ingredients as time goes on.

For a coordinate unit to succeed, it must lift the human spirit; at the same

131

time it must be economically feasible and follow a sensible, efficient plan. In addition to providing places for work, residence, shopping, and recreation, it must draw on all the elements that I have been discussing: a strong sense of order, complemented by a variety of incident and unexpected change; light and color, nature and water to soften the constructed environment and make it more humane; shared space; and opportunities for people to watch people and all that movement entails. There must be a total life involvement.

The Embarcadero Center in San Francisco is part of something that comes close to the coordinate ideal that I describe, as the adjacent Golden Gateway housing is directly related to the center's offices, shopping, hotel, and entertainment development. The credit for originating this project must go to the late Justin Herman, who as head of the San Francisco Redevelopment Authority made a lasting and significant contribution to his city. He was a great public servant and a great man. It takes strong dedication and unyielding perseverance to create meaningful improvements at the scale of a city.

The Embarcadero Center became a reality in large part because of the interest and commitment of David Rockefeller, who wished to create a development of lasting value in a location that was important to the future of San Francisco and who was willing to accept the higher risk and somewhat longer payback period that a project of this kind demands.

The Renaissance Center in Detroit represents an even more important opportunity to build a coordinate unit on a comprehensive scale, but there are serious problems that did not exist in Atlanta or San Francisco. In those two cities, we were building on existing economic strengths and were able to develop one step at a time. If anything were to be done in Detroit, however, it needed to be done in a hurry. The city does not have fifteen years to build up a coordinate unit step by step. We are counteracting weakness, not building on strength. The first stage had to be large enough to justify its own independent existence.

In the same way that David Rockefeller made the future of San Francisco a factor in his investment decision, Henry Ford and the other businessmen who are supporting the Renaissance Center are making this commitment because they feel that it is the best alternative for their city. Renaissance Center is a private enterprise contribution to the future of Detroit and its people. The great companies that are participating and investing in the project are not doing it out of the profit motive but for a deep concern for their city. This represents American business and our private enterprise system in one of their most noble and responsive efforts, one that I hope will become a prototype for businesses to follow in other cities.

Our cities are testimony to the fact that private solutions to private problems cannot produce a viable environment of benefit to our society. Private interests must help government maintain the health and vitality of our communities if our way of life with all its freedoms is going to survive.

The corporate business structure of this country must recognize that there is an urgent need for it to take a new position of public responsibility. Some companies have abandoned the cities to get away from all the urban problems. Others have sought the suburbs for trivial reasons, such as greater convenience to executive homes and golf courses. They take their tax base with them, leaving behind the seeds of unemployment, social unrest, and revolution.

In Detroit, under the enlightened leadership of Henry Ford, business has

recognized that its public responsibility calls for staying in the city and working for solutions, not for turning its back and running. Business leaders have subordinated company ego, and forgone individual identifying signboards, to build a new kind of urban center for people, a center that could not exist if these businesses were not willing to pool their strengths and go beyond the property lines and corporate objectives. They are seeking a stabilized community, knowing that no business can operate without social stability.

The Renaissance Center also represents a new kind of opportunity for the architect; and if an emerging social consensus creates more design situations at this scale, it is imperative that the architectural profession be prepared to deal with them.

Architects are already trained to take all kinds of different needs and requirements and design structures that will accommodate them all. They are also trained to synthesize the contributions of various specialists— mechanical and structural engineers, landscape designers, lighting

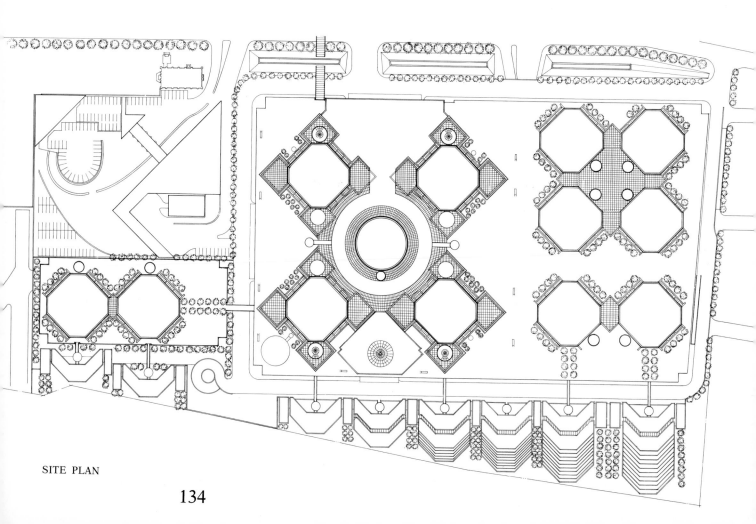

SITE PLAN

consultants, painters, sculptors—and bring all their work together into some kind of harmonious result. They become skilled coordinators of all these interests.

Because architects are accustomed to taking diverse elements and bringing them together into a single solution, I am confident that they have the qualifications to become master coordinators for the physical development of entire cities. Perhaps this sounds like a presumptuous statement. But what is a city? A city is structures that house people. Now what makes the city, the people or the structures? Well, both. But the architect, or physical designer, is the one who creates the environment: the things that we see, and the things that we use, as the city. Isn't it natural that the architect would be the one to prepare to orchestrate the city to the highest possible level, so that it contributes as much as possible to the elevation of human life and the ability of human beings to function within their environment?

Of course, architects have not been asked to do this very often, nor are they

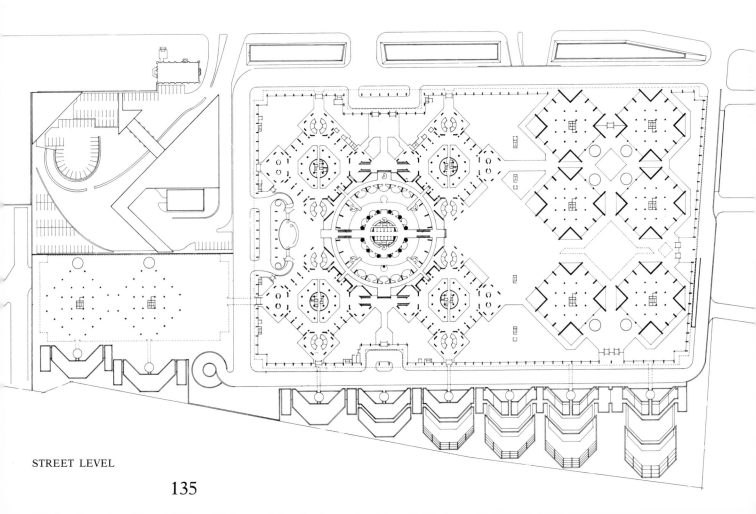

STREET LEVEL

at present trained to do so. If architects are to become master coordinators of cities, they must prove that they are able to do the job. First, of course, they must master their trade as architects. Then they must broaden their base to include all the factors that bring a building into being—what I call the building birth cycle.

If architects can anticipate the future by understanding growth patterns, if they understand real estate values, if they understand market conditions and market feasibilities, and if they understand the financial climate that makes it right to do something or not to do something, then they will be able to design the city and not just the individual buildings.

It is not that complicated. Architects must be conversant with the building process, from the germ of an idea being born in somebody's mind until the building is sitting there and operating; but this does not mean that they must be absolute experts in every step along the way. After all, architects are seldom expert in the more complex aspects of mechanical systems or in the calculations for sophisticated structures, but they know enough about

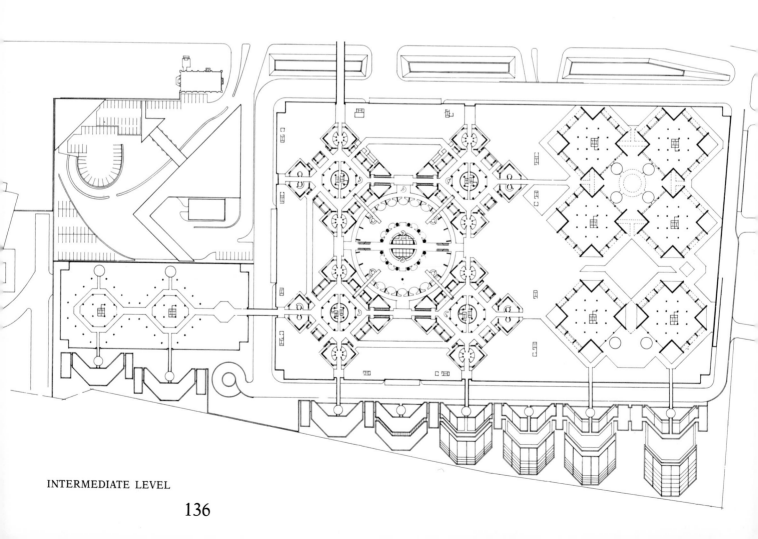

them to coordinate the work of consultants and incorporate their results in the final product. In the same way architects can use real estate consultants and the people who study market feasibility. They can also use financial advisers and legal advisers. To coordinate their work, architects must have enough understanding of all these things to put them together, just as they are accustomed to putting a building together.

There are many different ways for architects to play this coordinative role. They can work within government, like my colleague Jonathan Barnett and his fellow urban designers in New York. They could be advisers to insurance companies or other lenders. They could work for a consortium of business interests, as I am doing in Detroit, or from within the real estate development process, as I have done in Atlanta and other cities.

The opportunities are there if architects can learn how to use them. My own experience has led me to believe that it is not all that difficult for architects to expand their base and work to coordinate the physical environment.

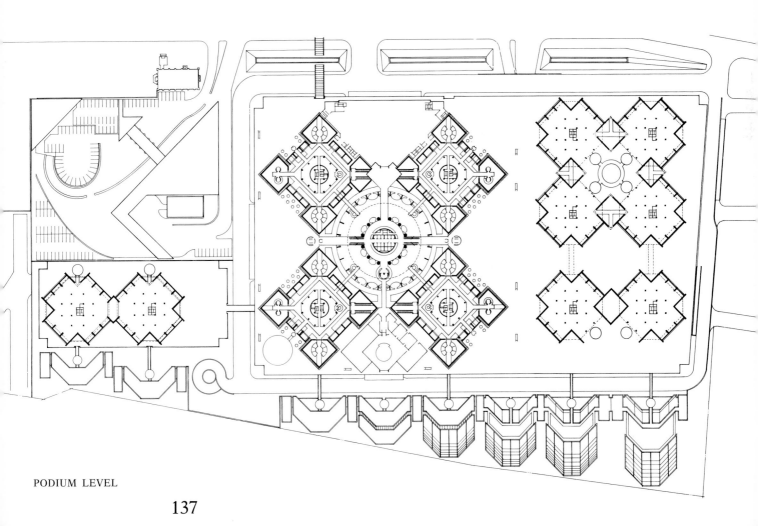

PODIUM LEVEL

137

*The central space
serves the hotel
and four office
towers.
Section elevation creates
a misleading
impression of the
spacing of the buildings,
which have been care-
fully handled and sited
to have a clear outlook
in all directions.*

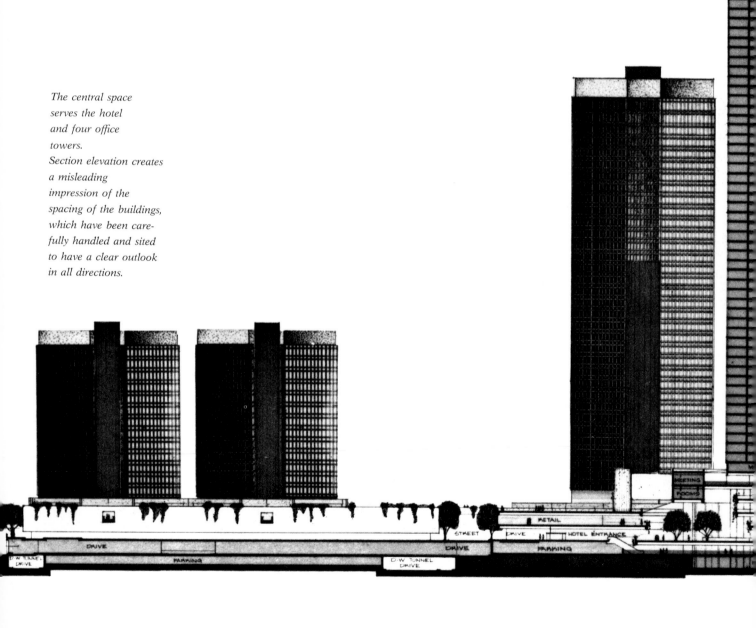

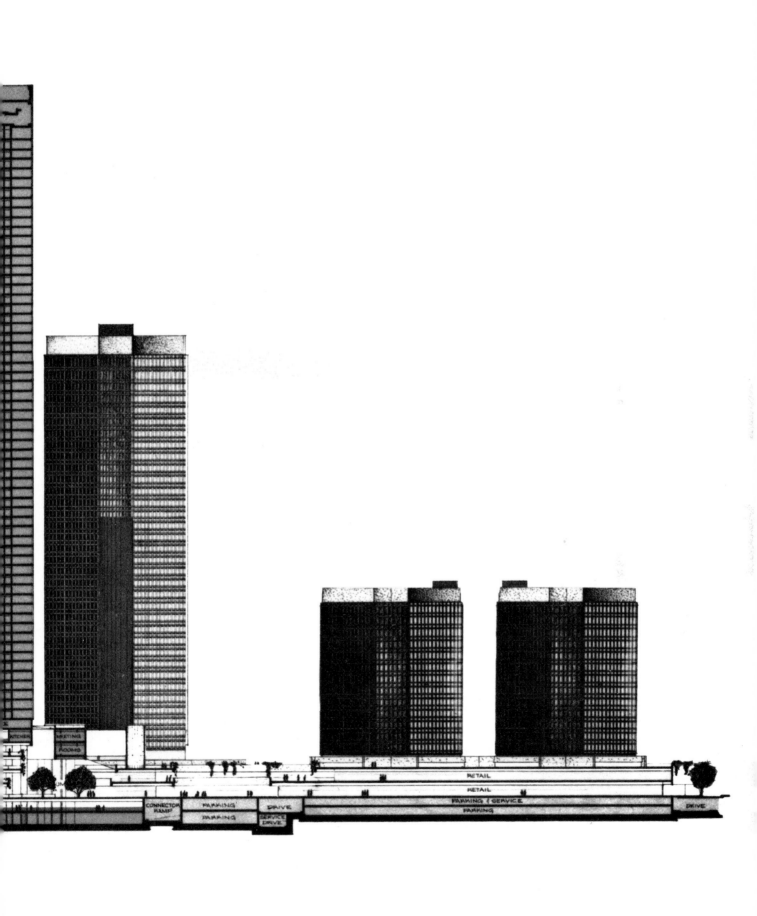

KITCHEN

MEETING
ROOMS

RETAIL

RETAIL

CONNECTOR
RAMP

PARKING

PARKING

DRIVE

SERVICE
DRIVE

PARKING / SERVICE

PARKING

DRIVE

APARTMENT ELEVATIONS LOOKING NORTH

ST. ANTOINE STREET ELEVATION LOOKING WEST

140

RANDOLPH STREET ELEVATION LOOKING EAST
SCALE: 1/16" = 1'-0"

JEFFERSON STREET ELEVATION LOOKING SOUTH
(TAKEN AT JEFFERSON AVE. BERA & MAIN PODIUM STRUCTURE)   SCALE: 1"=50'-0"

Instead of separate lobbies the hotel and office buildings have an integrated space that is a new kind of urban experience.

Part 3:   Architecture

as an investment

How architecture improves real estate —and the other way around

by Jonathan Barnett

John Portman uses the term "building birth cycle" to describe the long and complex process of which building design is just one part. The architect's role does not usually begin until many important decisions have been made about location, size, character, and budget. These decisions greatly restrict the number of alternatives open to the architect, and often assumptions have been made without any real understanding of their effect on design. If architects could participate in these early decisions, they could design better buildings; but for their suggestions to be taken seriously they must understand the other issues involved.

Portman defines seven aspects of the development process that architects must master to participate in all the critical decisions about a building:

1. The structural organization of the city and its existing growth pattern

2. The real estate market and the effect of design and cost on marketability

3. The preparation of studies that measure feasibility: economic, social, and political

4. Projections of total development cost, of which building cost is a substantial percentage but by no means the whole story

5. Projections of income and expenses over a long period of time, usually called the "financial pro forma"

6. The financial market and the ways to put together the financing of a building

7. The renting and operation of the completed building

Portman's organization has grown progressively, adding one real estate capability after another, until he has succeeded in combining architecture and real estate into a single, fully integrated operation. Each of the seven aspects of real estate development has significant implications for the design process, and design can have an important impact on real estate decisions as well.

Urban structure and growth patterns

The location and size of the property selected for a building clearly has a fundamental effect on its design. Is the land a hillside, or is it flat? Is the property long and narrow or short and wide? But these questions of land configuration are usually considered as subordinate to the position of the property within the intricate web of relationships that make up the functional organization of the city. Every city has a functional structure and established patterns of growth (or decay) that are well understood by the real estate business. As knowledge of these patterns is worth money, there is no rush to publicize them; but as the old saw goes, the three most important factors in real estate are location, location, and location.

For example, central business districts tend to grow by accretion, with each developer trying to locate his project next door to one that is already successful. This concept has been axiomatic for almost a century. The Monadnock Building in Chicago, completed in 1891,

148

was named for an isolated peak that stands at some distance from the rest of the White Mountains of New Hampshire—a wry comment on the building's somewhat risky location.

The planners of many urban renewal districts have apparently overlooked this basic observation about urban growth; and private developers, tempted by lower land prices and ease of assemblage, have been known to make the same error.

Portman has spent a lot of time walking around downtown areas, trying to understand their structure and dynamics. He does not believe that development away from an existing center is necessarily doomed to failure, but he thinks that the initial development in a new location must be large enough, and diverse enough, to succeed on its own.

Portman feels that the location he chose for the Atlanta Merchandise Mart, his first major project, was an absolutely critical element in its success and the subsequent success of Peachtree Center. It was near enough to a healthy, growing business center to profit by its activity and yet far enough away to permit assemblage of a large tract at a manageable cost, and step-by-step development.

Establishing the desirability of a location is an intuitive process akin to the mysterious mechanism by which an architect arrives at a concept for a building. It requires skillful observation and deduction and an understanding of the importance and relationships of factors that cannot be measured exactly. Sample question: do the advantages of overlooking a park outweigh the disadvantages of being two blocks farther away from a transit station?

But if location in the land use pattern of the city is more important than the characteristics of the land itself, the nature of a particular property is still important. The developer may be unaware that the kind of building he has in mind could be built more economically on a hillside or that the combination of a narrow site and the local zoning laws will make the floor areas of the building he proposes too small for certain uses. There is an interaction between building location and design, and rules of thumb or stereotyped assumptions can foreclose valuable alternatives.

Marketability

There is also an interaction between building design and marketability. However, as market studies are usually done long before there has been a decision to go ahead and design a building, the market analyst must make his own design assumptions. A logical assumption is that the building will be average; it will resemble the average apartment house, office building, or whatever, that has been built in the same general area over the last few years. As a result, there has been little investigation of the ways that changes in design might affect real estate marketability.

Not that market analysis is anything like an exact science even when it is dealing with established building concepts. While the results of a market study will be presented in a seemingly objective way, their production requires intuition and an understanding of intangibles.

The basis of a market study is some simple arithmetic: the number of families that live in a trading area; census data about age, occupation, income distribution; and the answers to other quantifiable questions, such as the number of established and potential competitors.

However, judgment must be used to reduce marketing issues to measurable quantities. What is a reasonable definition of a trading area? A five-minute walk? A twenty-minute drive? What percentage of potential customers in the trading area will actually use a certain kind of store? The answers to these questions come from observation and experience in other places, sometimes supplemented by questionnaires for the area under study as a basis for statistical projections.

A real estate developer ordinarily does not prepare his own market studies because he wants to convince potential lenders of the objectivity of his information. Portman realized quite early, however, that he would have to check the assumptions of the market analysts working on his projects. He wants allowances to be made for his intention to deliver a different and, he is certain, superior product. A hotel with a large and exciting interior space will operate with higher occupancy rates and room rents than a conventional market projection would indicate, the restaurants and bars will do a better-than-average volume of business, and so on.

Accustomed to making their evaluations before a building had actually been designed, the market analysts at first had trouble in taking architecture into their calculations. Now that there has been some experience with the way that Portman's hotels and other buildings actually perform in the market, it is relatively easy to incorporate their very favorable record into projections for the future. Portman has also affected the market, particularly for hotels, by demonstrating that the total environment is important, that an atmosphere of variety and excitement can have a beneficial effect on financial performance.

Feasibility

Economic feasibility is determined through projections of total cost and the financial pro forma, which we shall come back to shortly. Social and political feasibility are less easily measured but are equally important.

In these days of organized communities, complex zoning regulations, and environmental impact statements, a real estate developer must have a good understanding of the costs and benefits that his project creates for the community as a whole and be prepared to argue his case. The developer must spend a lot of time in working with community leaders and government officials. A project that makes economic sense may be politically infeasible because of its impact on various groups within the community.

Portman has the additional problem that many of his unconventional designs run afoul of local building codes. His office has become expert at working through the objections of local officials and resolving them through meticulous attention to detail. When architects run into trouble getting a large space approved, they often call up the Portman organization to find out how it can be done.

150

Total development cost

Having selected a potential location, made market studies, and determined that a project is socially and economically feasible, the developer must now make certain that the project he has in mind makes economic sense. He will naturally have been making financial calculations all along, but now he must be more precise. Some developers will bring an architect into the process at this point to make preschematic designs that form the basis for a takeoff of construction costs. All too often, however, the developer will use construction cost averages, based on the price for building similar structures in the same general area. If the site selection, market studies, and construction cost estimates are all based on averages, it is not surprising that the architect often ends up by having to design an average building.

ILLUSTRATIVE BUDGET FOR A 1,500-ROOM HOTEL WITH 100,000 SQUARE FEET OF RETAIL SPACE

PROJECT COST PRO FORMA For a construction period of thirty-one months.

1. Land	$ 7,000,000
2. Base Building	70,000,000
3. Architect's fee	4,200,000
4. Property tax during construction	2,000,000
5. Material testing	500,000
6. Project administration	1,500,000
7. Financial, legal, and closing	4,000,000
8. Technical consulting	400,000
9. Miscellaneous	1,700,000
10. Furniture, fixtures, and equipment	9,500,000
11. Retail space finish	1,500,000
12. Preopening and expendables	5,000,000
13. Contingency	6,000,000
14. Interim interest	8,000,000
Total	**$121,300,000**

The cost estimates used in working out the financing of one of Portman's buildings are always based on the actual design, which is carried far enough that accurate estimates can be made. This precision is a major reason why Portman has been able to build his unconventional designs.

Of course, building cost, while it is important, is not the only factor in determining total development cost, which for a Portman hotel will include fourteen categories of expenditure, as listed in the table shown above. Building construction represents something like three-fifths of the total money needed. There are four sets of fees, including the architect's fee and a project administration fee that goes to the developer. Both of these fees may go to a Portman organization, which is unusual, but they are standard parts of the cost of any building and are covered by the financing. There is also a budget for financial and legal fees, closing costs, and additional technical consulting fees, plus an additional item for materials testing.

Furniture, fittings, and equipment are also part of the total. Another item is an allowance for finishing the portion of the retail space that is the responsibility of the owner. The total project cost in a hotel also includes an allowance for preopening working capital (mostly for hotel staff salaries) and the "expendables" (food, liquor, paper goods,

151

and so on) needed to prepare the hotel for its first customers. There are additional miscellaneous and contingency items that represent about 4 percent of the total.

The projections for an office building will have different items on the list, but the principles are the same: the list must be exhaustive, and the implications of important variables—building and land costs, interim interest—must be understood as soon as possible.

Portman advises that no developer or owner should proceed with a project without a maximum construction price guaranteed by the contractor.

Projection of income and expenses

Once total cost has been determined, the next step in analyzing feasibility is to see if projected income, after expenses, can pay back the development costs and provide an appropriate profit.

In a hotel, occupancy and room rates are variables and are projected to rise as the hotel becomes established. The rise in room rates is also predicated partly on inflation. Food and beverage income and income from other sources (parking, meeting rooms, laundry, valet, health club) are also projected, giving an estimate of gross operating revenue for representative years after the hotel opens (see table opposite).

The operating expenses are estimated on the same long-range basis, making allowance for inflation. They include administrative, advertising, and promotion costs as well as the expenses of operating the rooms, restaurants, and other areas. The sum of these costs, subtracted from the gross operating revenues, gives the gross operating profit. (Obviously, if there should be a negative figure at this stage, something is very wrong.)

As the Portman organization arranges its pro forma, annual insurance premiums and real estate taxes are deducted from the gross operating profit, and a net profit figure from the hotel's retailing operation is added, giving a net income before fees and reserve. The fee in this case is the annual figure paid to the hotel management company that operates the hotel.

After the operating fee and reserve allowance are subtracted, you are left with the sum of money available to pay back principal and interest of a mortgage loan and provide what developers call "cash flow."

Financing

Developers almost never finance a whole project out of their own resources; they are entrepreneurs merchandising their ingenuity and experience, not financial institutions looking for places to put their money. If the big financial institutions, like insurance companies, were to act as developers themselves, the story would be different; but as Albert Mayer, the architect and planner, once wrote, the developer tail wags the investment dog.

The developer must look for two different kinds of financing: the construction loan, which pays for labor, materials, and other con-

ILLUSTRATIVE OPERATING

Attained transient rate
Occupancy

Gross operating revenue

    Rooms
    Food and beverage
    Telephone
    Laundry and valet
    Health club and pool
    Hotel retail: net
    Parking
    Total gross revenues

Cost of sales

    Rooms
    Food and beverage
    Telephone
    Laundry and valet
    Health club and pool
    Parking
    Total costs

Other operating expenses

    General and administrative
    Advertising and promotion
    Maintenance and utilities
    Total other
    Total operating expenses

Gross operating profit

Fixed expense

    Insurance
    Real estate tax
    Total fixed expenses
    Net house profit

Other revenues

    Shopping gallery
    Theater

Net before fees and reserves

struction costs as they are incurred; and the permanent mortgage and other permanent financing, which are used to pay back the construction loan after the building is complete and which then are paid back over a long term of years.

The bottom-line figure from the projection of income and expenses is the money available to pay interest on borrowed money and repay the principal. It thus becomes the basis on which the value of the building is determined for lending purposes. It is extremely important to remember that the value of a building is related to income and not to construction cost. An inexpensive structure that returns a high income may easily be worth more than it cost to build; an expensive building with no foreseeable use will be worth almost nothing. If

PRO FORMA FOR A 1,500-ROOM CONVENTION HOTEL

Year 1		Year 2		Stabilized year	
$40.00 72%		$45.00 78%		$53.50 82%	
Ratio (%)	($000)	Ratio (%)	($000)	Ratio (%)	($000)
45.3	15,768	47.1	19,217	48.2	24,019
49.7	17,300	47.9	19,543	46.8	23,321
1.8	626	1.9	775	1.9	947
1.2	418	1.2	490	1.2	598
.2	69	.2	82	.2	100
.7	244	.6	245	.6	299
1.1	383	1.1	448	1.1	548
100.0	34,808	100.0	40,800	100.0	49,832
13.1	4,560	12.2	4,978	11.1	5,531
41.2	14,341	35.9	14,647	34.1	16,993
2.7	940	2.6	1,061	2.7	1,345
1.0	348	.9	367	.8	399
.3	104	.2	82	.2	100
.3	104	.3	122	.3	149
58.6	20,397	52.1	21,257	49.2	24,517
6.0	2,088	5.6	2,285	5.0	2,492
3.3	1,149	3.1	1,265	3.0	1,495
7.6	2,645	7.3	2,978	7.0	3,488
16.9	5,882	16.0	6,528	15.0	7,475
75.5	26,279	68.1	27,785	64.2	31,992
24.5	**8,529**	**31.9**	**13,015**	**35.8**	**17,840**
.4	139	.3	140	.3	149
10.6	3,690	11.1	4,529	10.8	5,382
11.0	3,829	11.4	4,669	11.1	5,531
13.5	4,700	20.5	8,346	24.7	12,309
5.4	1,880	5.2	2,122	5.0	2,492
.1	35	.2	81	.2	100
19.0	**6,615**	**25.9**	**10,549**	**29.9**	**14,901**

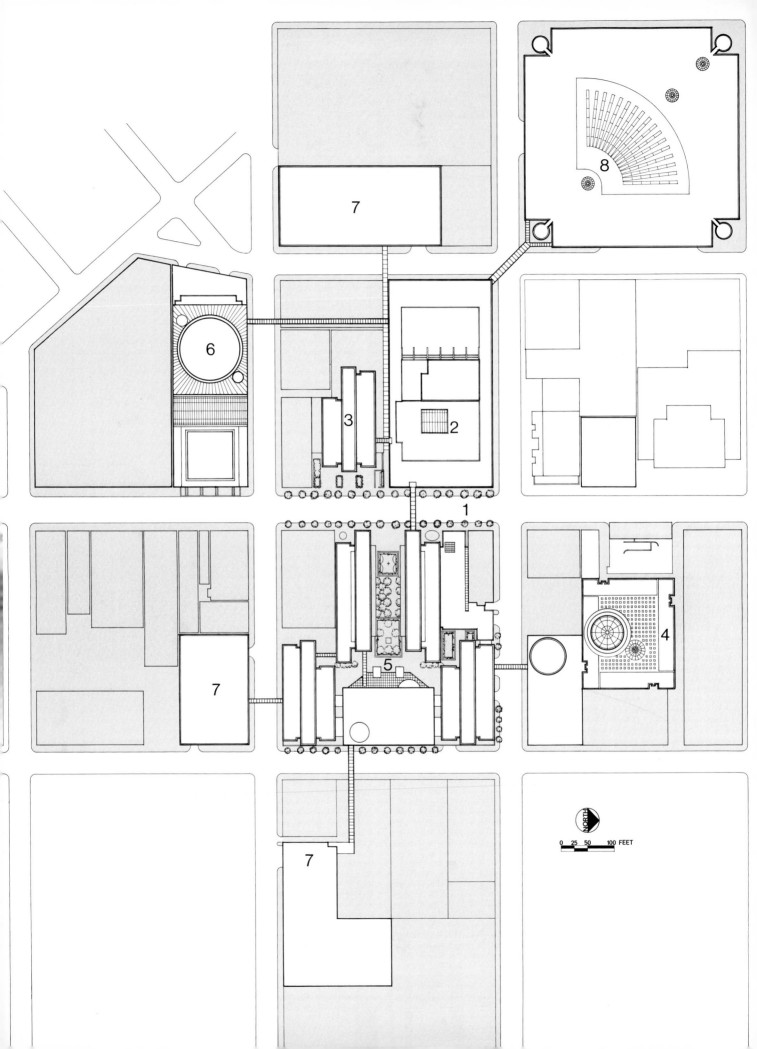

1

2

3

4

5

6

7

7

7

8

0 25 50   100 FEET

NORTH

such an expensive building is on valuable land, it may make economic sense to tear it down. Many an old mansion is in this category. Its owner may have lavished millions on it, but if no one can afford to live in it today and no institution wants it, the real estate value will be much less than its original cost.

A permanent lender can give a first mortgage of up to 75 percent of the building's value. Where the remaining money comes from is a function of the developer's ingenuity and market conditions. As a general principle, the developer wants to own as much of the building as he can with as little of his own equity invested as possible. Two of the alternatives: he can find a second mortgage, or he can sell equity participation in the building. Under the second alternative the investor becomes a part owner (the percentage is a matter of negotiation) and thus owns a percentage of the building's expenses and losses that is deductible for income tax purposes.

Site plan shows Peach-
tree Center today:
(1) Peachtree Street;
(2) the Merchandise Mart;
(3) the first Peachtree
Center office building;
(4) the Hyatt Regency
Atlanta hotel;
(5) the main Peachtree
Center office complex,
courtyards, Shopping
Gallery, and dinner
theater; (6) the Peach-
tree Plaza Hotel;
(7) parking garages; and
(8) the Apparel Mart.

Portman makes a point of not going out to seek permanent financing until he knows exactly how much money he needs and precisely why he needs it. Because his buildings are unconventional, he is careful to make his financial projections as nearly complete as possible, and his projects are financed because of their advantages as real estate, not because of their architecture.

The permanent lenders will not make their investment until the building has been completed. Once permanent financing has been secured, the developer is in a position to obtain the interim financing, the construction loan. This loan covers costs until the "takeout" occurs, the money being drawn down as it is required during construction.

Management

Portman is a developer who wishes to hold his buildings for the long term. To do that, he must be able to convince a permanent lender that he has the capability to operate his buildings for the life of the mortgage. In the case of the Peachtree Plaza and Los Angeles hotels, Portman has an operating agreement with Western International, a highly respected hotel company. Peachtree and Embarcadero Centers each have their own management entities, and the Merchandise Marts run their own operations. Management is not an afterthought but an essential element in Portman's long-range plans.

Obviously the road from location and basic concept decisions to the management of the completed building is not a simple linear progression. There are a lot of what systems analysts call feedback loops along the way, points in the process where things do not come out right, and it is necessary to go back and do work over or to change assumptions. The most important conceptual decisions in real estate and architecture, as in other areas, remain intuitive in nature, no matter how detailed the information on which they are based or how precise their evaluation later. Portman makes almost all the conceptual decisions himself, and his office organization has evolved as a rigorous counterbalance, testing his ideas to make sure that they will work.

Portman's role is to understand the specific situation in as much detail

155

as possible. His model is the scientist who seeks the most elegant and definitive statement of the problem in order to achieve the correct or appropriate solution. Portman, on his own, will work out a design or real estate concept. He will then advocate it, and it is up to his associates to help him test it to see if it works. If he becomes convinced that his initial idea was wrong, he will abandon it and go back to the drawing board, seeking a better solution.

Portman never loses sight of his role as an architect despite his immersion in real estate marketability, finance, and management; by mastering the context in which he must work, he is enhancing the depth of his understanding of architecture.

As an example of the way in which Portman and his organization operate, let us take the development and design of the Peachtree Plaza Hotel, the cylindrical building that is the latest addition to Peachtree Center, and follow its chronology step by step.

The story begins when the lease on the land under the old Henry Grady Hotel came up for renewal. The hotel stood on Peachtree Street, just a block south of the Merchandise Mart. The land belonged to the state of Georgia; it had once been the site of the Governor's Mansion. As the land was public property, the state advertised for bids on the terms of a new ninety-nine-year lease in January 1969.

Portman's decision to acquire control of this property was an intuitive one, based on his exceptionally detailed knowledge of the downtown Atlanta real estate market. Portman had been studying the properties around the mart for years; he knew the size, value, and ownership of every parcel and when and if each one was likely to come on the market. He knew that the Henry Grady property was the largest site on his part of Peachtree Street that would become available. The hotel had an interesting history as a political meeting place, but it was an undistinguished and run-down structure that Portman felt was ripe for redevelopment. He was sure that Peachtree Center still had plenty of potential for future growth, and he had learned that expansion was blocked in several other directions. He also did not wish any other developer to gain control of the property and produce something out of harmony with Peachtree Center. Instead, Portman wished to extend the designed environment he was creating toward Atlanta's historical and traditional center, down Peachtree Street south to Five Points.

To Portman, these reasons were decisive. He did not need a market study; in fact, at this point he had no clear idea what use he would make of the property. Of course, considerable time and effort went into calculating the terms of the bid: enough to secure the property but not so much as to put a heavy burden on future development. A bid for the lease was made by the Jamestown Shopping Center, Inc., an existing legal entity set up and jointly owned by Portman and Trammell Crow.

Although many copies of the official documents had been requested by potential bidders, Portman's Jamestown bid was the only one actually made. In the chaotic last moments of the 1969 session of the Legislature, Portman's lawyer, Travis Brannon of Hansell, Post,

Brandon and Dorsey, was able to secure the passage of a bill giving him the lease.

The lawyer's mission was to acquire control of the property, and he had done so. He warned Portman, however, that the best he had been able to do was not good enough: the terms of the lease were probably not mortgageable; that is, no permanent lender would finance a building on the property. Portman was disappointed but not overly concerned, because he knew it was in the state's best interest as well as his own to see the property developed. The lease did not begin to run until 1972, and he was confident that he could modify it when the time came.

The decision to use the Henry Grady site for a new and much larger hotel was also an intuitive and conceptual one. It may have been influenced by Portman's regret at having to sell his first Peachtree Center hotel, the Regency, to Hyatt. Portman was also disappointed by the way some of Hyatt's managers were running the Regency, which he did not feel lived up to the standards he was trying to establish for Peachtree Center. Much of the decor made him grind his teeth, and the hotel was so popular that the management was able to operate at a level of service and cleanliness which was certainly below that of a first-class establishment. (Later, as the hotel business in Atlanta became more competitive, Hyatt brought in a new manager and completely refurbished the hotel.)

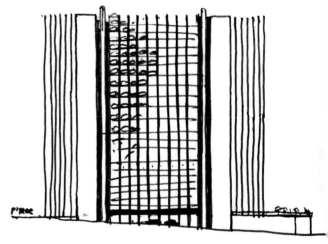

Portman could rely on Atlanta's new convention center to provide a market for additional hotel rooms, but many other new hotels were planned or in construction. The initial market studies, done by a consultant, were not encouraging. Nonetheless, Portman did not accept their results. He felt that the consultants were going by typical development rules of thumb for predicting marketability, while it was his plan to capture the top of the market by sharing the role of the Hyatt Regency Atlanta. His experience with the hotels he had de-signed in Atlanta, Chicago, and San Francisco also led him to believe that the pulling power of his buildings created a higher-than-average income from shops and food and beverage operations. When all these points were explained, the consultants reconsidered the hotel's feasibility and produced a more favorable report.

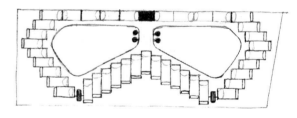

First parti of hotel was a figure-eight pattern.

The real estate study did give Portman some important design con-straints. He was convinced that the hotel, in order to draw the best convention business, needed to have approximately 1,200 rooms as well as a long list of meeting and exhibition rooms that would take up a great deal of space. The Henry Grady site was not large, less than $1\frac{1}{2}$ acres, or 56,000 square feet. Could a hotel of the size required fit on the site? It was time to find out.

It was at this point, in September 1969, that Portman first began to work on the architectural design of this project. His initial idea was to build the hotel around another large atrium, a bigger version of the Hyatt Regency hotel. The difficulty was that one of the long sides of the site, blocked by the wall of Davison's department store, could not be used for hotel rooms below the eighth story. To minimize the effects of the blank wall, Portman tried undulating the opposite long wall, giving the hotel something of a figure-eight pattern and creating a major new difficulty: the closely spaced supports for the hotel

157

rooms would come down on top of the exhibit and meeting spaces, which needed large open areas unobstructed by columns. However, it was clear that a hotel of the scope that Portman wanted could be designed on the site somehow, and he left the design for the time being to work on other projects.

In April 1970, Portman came back to the design of the Henry Grady site with another alternative, carrying all the hotel rooms in a huge A-frame structure that would leave unobstructed spaces for the convention areas. But the A frame created nasty problems of its own, particularly for the fire stairs, mechanical risers, and shafts, which would have to be offset on every floor, as well as being an expensive structural solution.

In June 1970, Portman left his design staff to struggle with the A frame and went off on one of his rare vacation trips. As he cruised about the Greek islands, he came to the conclusion that the whole idea of the atrium was wrong: all the hotel rooms should center in a compact cylindrical structure, leaving the lower floors clear for the convention facilities and providing a spatial antithesis to the other Peachtree Center hotel, the Hyatt Regency.

The A-frame idea was shelved, but it is related to Portman's proposal for a Times Square hotel in New York, which was designed for a larger site that had only one short side obstructed by adjacent buildings, making the idea much more workable.

By April 1971 the cylindrical hotel had been worked out in sufficient detail that real cost figures could be provided by the building contractor, the J. A. Jones Construction Co., which had been selected to build the hotel on a negotiated, guaranteed-cost contract.

The figures permitted a much more realistic development cost budget to be worked up by Portman's feasibility study consultant, Peat-Marwick-Mitchell & Company. These figures in turn permitted three important steps to take place. Negotiations could start with hotel companies on an operating lease, Portman could go out to seek financing, and the process of modifying the lease with the state could begin.

In the meantime, the architectural office went on developing the design in detail and producing the drawings and specifications from which the hotel would actually be built.

In May 1971 a structural analysis was done to compare the economics of building the frame of the hotel in steel or in concrete. Although the construction time for the concrete frame was slower, overall time to complete the building was about the same, and concrete was selected for cost reasons. By early June, major organizational and planning problems had been solved, although when the operating agreement was signed with Western International Hotels Inc., some changes in the floor plans were requested to improve operations.

In January 1972 the working drawings were begun. By May 8 these were complete enough for a firm building cost proposal from the contractor, and a letter of intent was signed on May 15, 1972. The building permit was issued in January 1973, final arrangements for financing were made, and construction began in May. The building

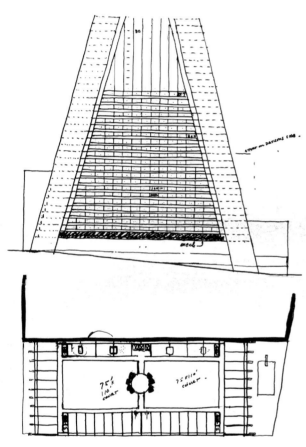

Second parti was a gigantic A frame, which created serious technical problems. Both sketches by John Portman.

Portman's sketches for the concept that became the final design.

A conference in the drafting room. Portman is talking to John Street, who has been his associate since the days of his first architectural office. At left is Portman's son John C. Portman III, who joined the office as an architect in 1974. At right is another longtime Portman associate, Herbert Lembcke.

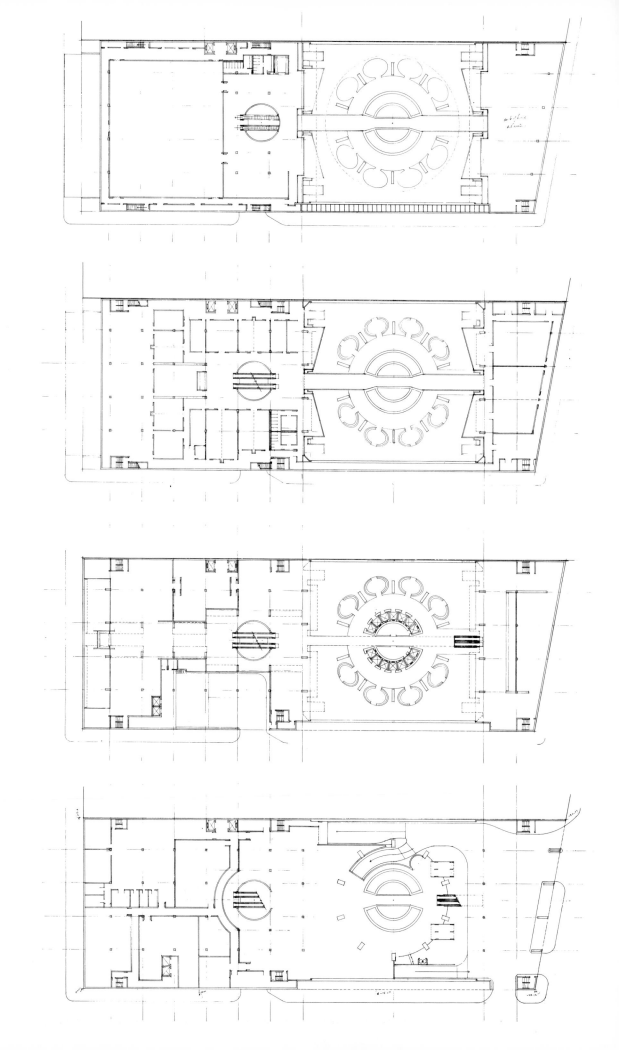

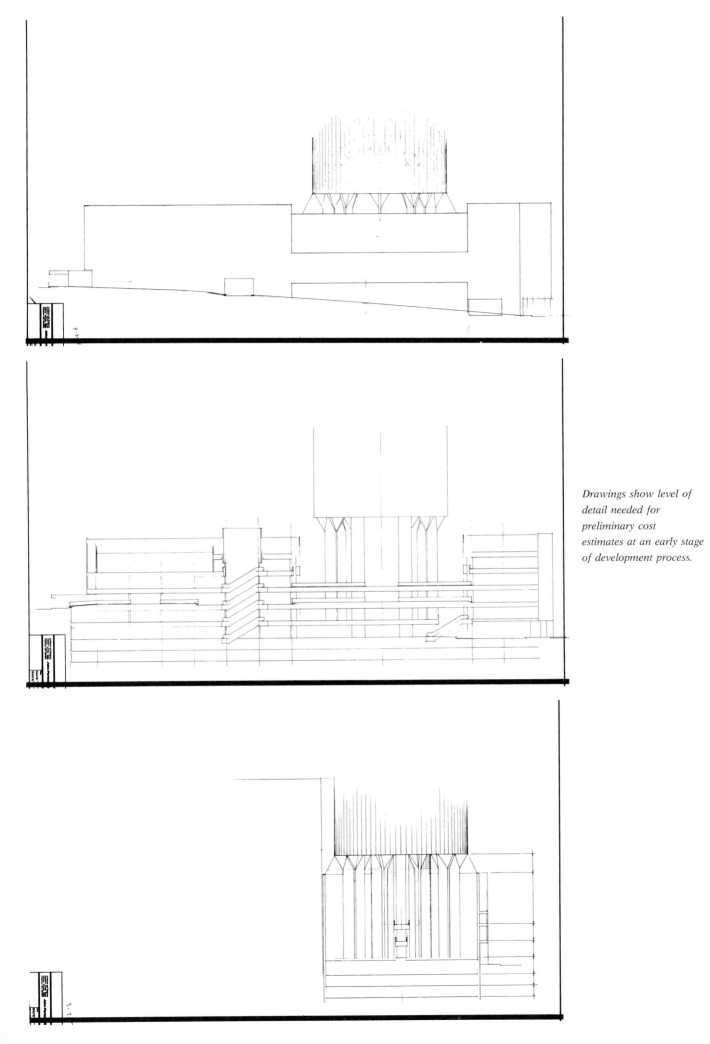

Drawings show level of detail needed for preliminary cost estimates at an early stage of development process.

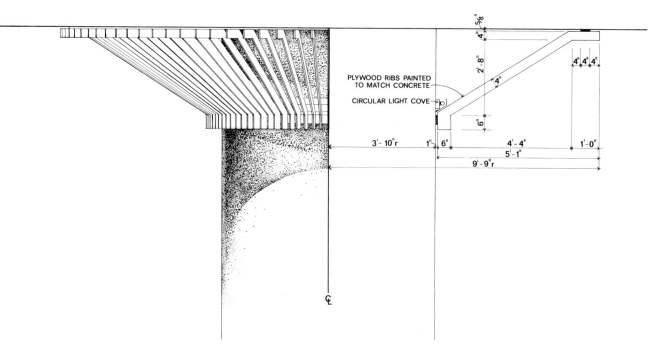

PLYWOOD RIBS PAINTED TO MATCH CONCRETE

CIRCULAR LIGHT COVE

5⁄8"

4"

2'- 8"

4"

6"

4" 4" 4"

4"

3'- 10"r

1"

6"

4'- 4"

1'- 0"

5'- 1"

9'- 9"r

℄

was completed, on schedule, in January 1976, within 2 percent of its estimated budget.

Portman's involvement in the design during this period was constant but varied with the nature of the task. He took a directing role in determining the concept, the structure, and the arrangement of major spaces, and he did all of the interior design himself. From this point on, as the team proceeded with the detailed development of the drawings, he checked back frequently, giving direction and supervision.

Portman will use any time that is not scheduled for important meetings to work his way through the drafting room, going from one project to another, checking on the progress of each one and answering questions as they come up. On a Saturday he will have uninterrupted time to review the progress of each building. His key staff will be on hand, and there is time for long discussions about the philosophy of design.

Detail of the way column capitals meet the top of the main space, expressing support for the hotel above but in a clearly nonstructural way.

Like many serious architects, Portman has a highly developed ability to visualize what his buildings will look like. Just as an orchestral conductor can look at a score and hear all the instruments, Portman can look at a drawing and not only see the spaces in three dimensions but mentally walk through them. Because he sees it all so clearly, he sometimes takes it for granted that everyone else understands what he has in mind. The people who work with him have learned to piece out his descriptions with inferences of their own, but, naturally, there are failures of communication. There are also occasions when Portman has not visualized something as clearly as he thought he did. Usually these problems are caught while still in the drawing stage, but sometimes they find their way into the completed building. While a building will serve its basic purpose even if the proportions of floor and wall finishes are not coordinated, a fully realized work of architecture requires virtual perfection of detail. Portman's complex schedule compromises his ability to control every detail of the design, although this is a difficulty familiar to any architect who has more than one or two major buildings in his office at the same time.

Portman certainly wants every detail to be as close to perfection as he can bring it. One device, which his office uses frequently, is to take a successful detail from one job and use it again when analogous situations require it. Portman takes a great interest in criticizing past mistakes and seeing that they are not repeated, and he is as much interested in the layout of a restaurant banquette or the design of a lighting fixture as he is in basic conceptual decisions. In the Peachtree Plaza Hotel he devoted a great deal of attention to the way in which the structural columns met the top of the main space, finally settling on an arrangement of lighting baffles which plays the role of a classic column capital by expressing support of the tower above but, unlike a column capital, in a nonstructural way.

There is a story about these columns which illustrates Portman's propensity to continue seeking improvements in a design even after construction has begun. His original intent had been to cover the columns with mirrors, but, after the concrete had been poured, he decided that the mirrors would be a bad idea. They would deprive the viewer of a full sense of the structure, destroying the meaning of

163

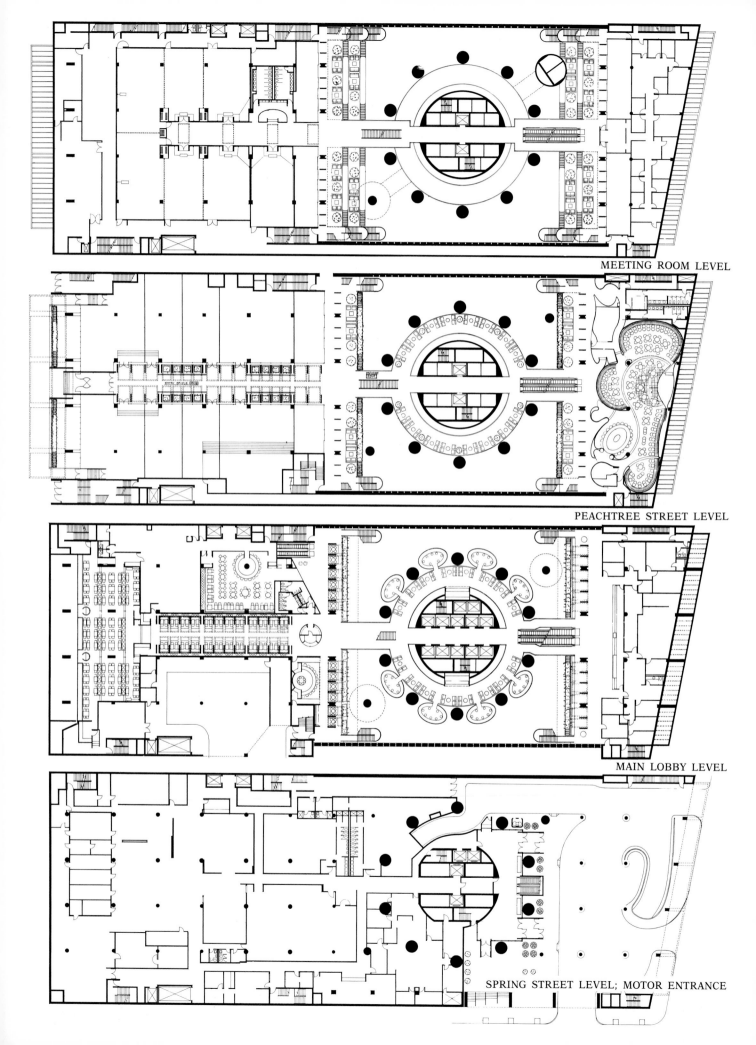

MEETING ROOM LEVEL

PEACHTREE STREET LEVEL

MAIN LOBBY LEVEL

SPRING STREET LEVEL; MOTOR ENTRANCE

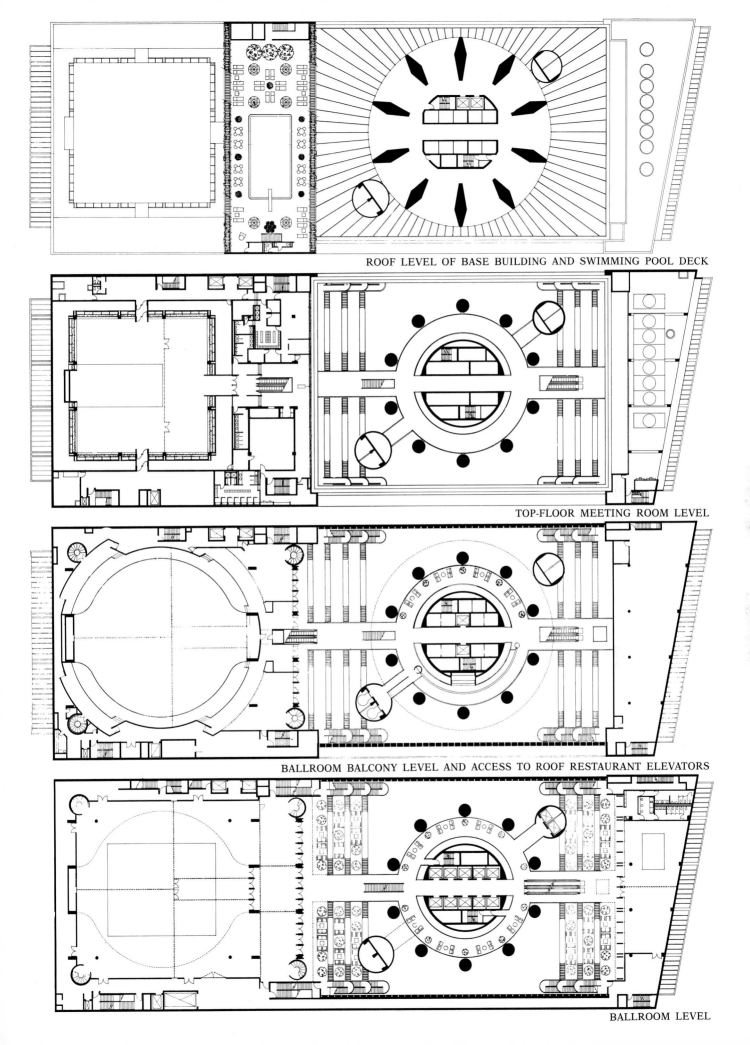

ROOF LEVEL OF BASE BUILDING AND SWIMMING POOL DECK

TOP-FLOOR MEETING ROOM LEVEL

BALLROOM BALCONY LEVEL AND ACCESS TO ROOF RESTAURANT ELEVATORS

BALLROOM LEVEL

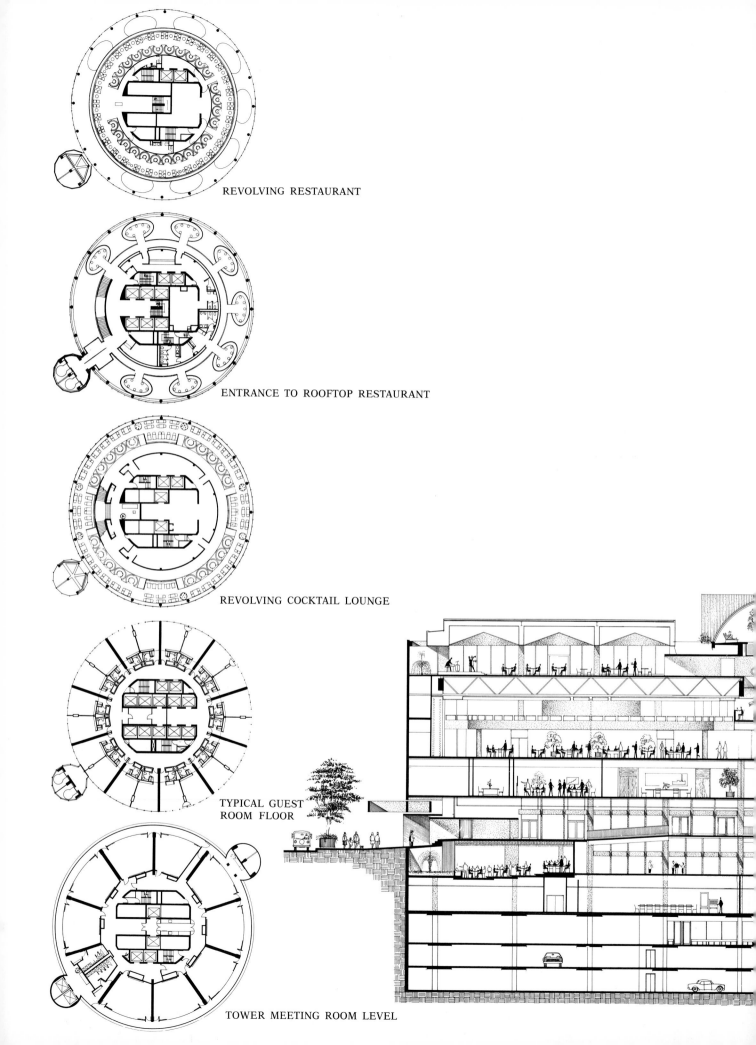

REVOLVING RESTAURANT

ENTRANCE TO ROOFTOP RESTAURANT

REVOLVING COCKTAIL LOUNGE

TYPICAL GUEST
ROOM FLOOR

TOWER MEETING ROOM LEVEL

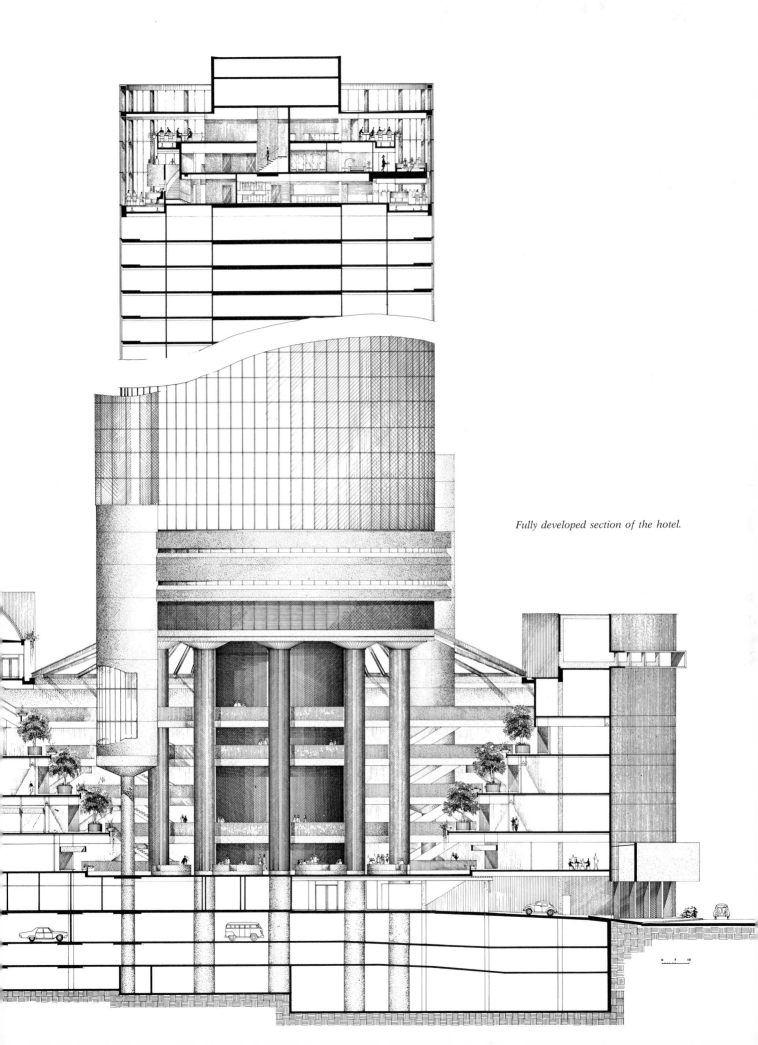

Fully developed section of the hotel.

The hotel tower dominates the Atlanta skyline. Bronze glass windows of the top-floor restau[rant] levels interrupt the mirrored sur[face] and give a subtle termination to [the] building.

the space. Unfortunately, the mirrors had already been ordered; fortunately, there are many uses for mirrors in a hotel. Portman and his interior designers were able to work most of them into the decor in places where mirrors would have been used in any case.

The nature of the design process is such that second thoughts and revisions are inevitable; but the architect is generally powerless to do much about them unless he can convince the owner that the changes are worth making. Portman controlled the ownership of the Peachtree Plaza Hotel; so he had only to convince himself. His most comprehensive second thought, however, concerned the exterior wall panels of the hotel at the Embarcadero Center in San Francisco, in which Portman had two joint-venture partners, the contract had been let, and construction had begun. Intensive staff work made the substitution possible at only a nominal increase in building cost, approximately $\frac{6}{100}$ of 1 percent.

Portman takes a role on the financial side of a building analogous to the one he assumes in developing the design: he sets the basic concepts and works with his staff on the details. This meant that it was Portman himself who made the major approaches to state officials about amending the lease on the Henry Grady site, went to potential lenders about financing, and met with hotel companies to discuss operating arrangements.

The amended lease, in a form acceptable to permanent lenders, was approved by the Georgia Legislature in April 1972, to the surprise of a good many observers who were sure that this couldn't be done. The change was possible because Portman was able to convince all con-

168

The Peachtree Street facade of the hotel is deliberately self-effacing to blend with neighboring commercial buildings. The 230 Peachtree Street tower and the Merchandise Mart can be seen in the background.

cerned that it was in their best interests. The alternatives were a $56 million new hotel or, if the lease were not modified, a $3 million remodeled building. The new hotel meant a big increase in ad valorem taxes for the state, and it would raise the city's income from taxes on the property as well as being a major generator of convention business, which would help the city's economy in general. As a result, Portman had the support of the mayor and the city's delegation in the Legislature and was able to put together the votes necessary to modify the lease.

While Portman was working on the Atlanta hotel, he was at one stage or another in the development of four others: in Detroit (Detroit Plaza at Renaissance Center), in New York (Times Square), in Los Angeles (Bonaventure at Bunker Hill), and in Washington (Rosslyn, Virginia). He wanted to work with a hotel operating company that would feel as strongly about service and management as he does about design, and he preferred to see all the hotels operated by the same company.

Portman was able to negotiate an operating agreement covering all the hotels with Western International, whose progressive management was enthusiastic about Portman's designs. (The Rosslyn project ran into a negative zoning decision and was never built, and the Times Square hotel probably will not be built either.)

With the lease amended, his construction estimates firm, and an operator lined up, Portman then went out to seek his permanent financing. The first mortgage was shared by the Metropolitan Life Insurance Company and the Citizens' and Southern Real Estate

169

Investors. The Chase Real Estate Investment Trust provided second mortgage financing.

With additional ingenious arrangements, Portman was able to "mortgage out," that is, to borrow all the funds necessary to cover the total development cost. Portman's equity in the project thus consists of the expenses connected with developing the concept and making the financial arrangements, approximately $2 million between 1969 and 1973.

The construction loan was provided by a consortium of banks headed by the Chase Manhattan Bank of New York.

All these financial negotiations took a great deal of Portman's own time. Naturally, he relies on his staff to help him prepare for meetings, but he cannot afford to disregard details, as he is responsible for them. His associate in charge of real estate finance says: "He does his homework. Only rarely will a point come up in a meeting that he hasn't considered beforehand."

Portman also must participate personally in other meetings because his presence has important symbolic value. For example, in April 1972 he met with all the prospective subcontractors for the Peachtree Plaza Hotel to assure them that it was a real project and to ask them to hold their prices while he finished arrangements for the permanent financing. The content of the meeting could have been handled by the staff, but Portman's presence was necessary to make his commitment credible.

The great demands on Portman's time lend critical importance to his

*From the Peachtree Street
entrance of the hotel a
long, narrow walkway
with shops on either side
leads to the main space.
To increase the contrast
between the constricted
space of the approach
and the bold expanses of
the main room, the direct
view of the space is blocked
by a wall covered with a
tapestry. Only when you
step around this wall is
the full space revealed.*

office organization, an organization that is still evolving. The chronology of the Peachtree Plaza Hotel shows the ways in which Portman is involved at each stage of the development process, but it does not represent a typical pattern. Market conditions and circumstances differ from project to project. Because the redevelopment authorities in San Francisco required a hotel to be part of the Embarcadero Center project, Portman had to design a hotel that would succeed in a high-risk location which he might not have chosen himself. Development costs were higher, and the operating agreement was less favorable, so that the hotel has taken longer than usual to turn the corner and start making profits for its investors. The Bonaventure Hotel in Los Angeles has a much higher degree of equity financing than the Peachtree Plaza Hotel, because it was financed at a relatively unfavorable time in the money markets. Each project must meet its own set of circumstances in its own time frame.

The design and development period for the Peachtree Plaza Hotel, roughly from 1969 to 1973, was a time of important growth and change in the Portman organization. A most important element of change was the ending of the business relationship between Portman and Trammell Crow.

Portman's association with Crow, which began when Crow bought into the Merchandise Mart soon after its completion, was a beneficial one for both. It made an important difference to Portman's growth as a real estate developer. Crow was Portman's partner for the 230 Peachtree Building, the first hotel, and the initial two office structures on the Whitehead property, as well as the Jamestown Shopping

171

Center in suburban Atlanta, the Embarcadero Center venture in San Francisco, several projects in Texas, and the Merchandise Mart in Brussels. Portman was the architect for all these projects, which must have introduced Crow to new ideas about design. And Crow, in turn, gave Portman the benefit of experienced advice about real estate from one of the nation's largest developers.

In 1969, at the time that Portman and Crow made a bid for the Henry Grady site through their jointly owned Jamestown Shopping Center, Inc., Portman and Crow's interests were beginning to diverge. Crow did not share Portman's continuing commitment to Peachtree Center as a laboratory for a new kind of urban coordinate unit, and he was much less enthusiastic than Portman about the possibilities of the hotel site. Crow left it to Portman to develop the hotel on his own.

As time went on, other points of difference between Portman and Crow began to emerge. Crow is primarily a developer, while Portman is also the proprietor of an architectural office. Crow felt that Portman's fees were too high; he had been used to getting architectual services for less money. Portman felt that Crow did not understand that comprehensive design required more time and effort than routine, time-tested solutions.

Portman kept adding to his own in-house real estate capabilities, and Crow worked more and more with other architects. It became evident that the two organizations were no longer complementary and that they were growing in separate directions. Portman and Crow agreed to divide their investments; this process was completed at the end of 1973.

Portman found that his association with Crow had been rewarding; it had provided a kind of tempering, enabling him to test his own abilities alongside one of the most effective developers in the business. On his own, Portman has proved to be an increasingly conservative investor. The original Hyatt Regency hotel looks in retrospect to have been an incredibly risky investment. Portman must be a persuasive man to have induced associates who owned 80 percent of the project to commit themselves to the construction of a $20 million building of unprecedented design before adequate permanent financing was secured and without an operator for the hotel. Of course, the early 1960s in Atlanta were an optimistic economic period, and as it turned out, Portman was completely right about the potential of the hotel.

The Peachtree Plaza Hotel is much more conservatively financed. Portman's major period of risk was during the actual construction process, as it would be for any developer. A year's delay, such as was encountered by the original Hyatt Regency, adds a year's interest on that portion of the construction loan that has been drawn down, and there is no offsetting income.

Once the construction period was past, Portman's risk was restricted to his actual investment in the building, as each building is separately capitalized and is not tied to his other interests. As mentioned earlier, he had borrowed the total funds (he feels this is necessary if he is to continue building projects), and his investment consists only of the time and expenses of arranging the deal and architectural costs not covered by the fee.

174

The two exterior elevators that go to the rooftop restaurant are reached from the fifth level of the main space. An elevator is shown waiting to receive passengers in its windowed shaft. The dramatic, "world of tomorrow" appearance is an important aspect of the hotel's design. Portman has brought to life some of the drawings of the science fiction illustrators. At the same time, the strange spaces created are not in any way overwhelming because intimate, everyday places are provided as observation posts.

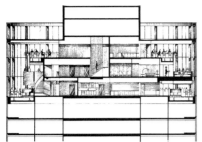

The rooftop restaurant has three levels. You enter at the intermediate floor, and either walk up to a revolving cocktail lounge or down to the dining space, which also revolves. Boat-shaped balconies at the intermediate level echo the islands on the lobby floor. As your dining table revolves, you alternately are under a balcony or the full, three-story height, so that your space changes as well as the view.

The connection to Davison's department store is from the Peachtree Street level. This link is an important aspect of the way Peachtree Center helps pull downtown Atlanta together into a new set of relationships. Below, the registration desk at the back of the main space.

Escalators from the motor entrance bring you up facing the desk. It is only when you turn around that you receive a glimpse of the main space.

One of the suites at the top of the tower. The decor
is by Western International, in consultation with
Portman. Below, the nightclub, done entirely in red.
This space, like all the public spaces in the hotel,
was designed by Portman.

Above, the coffee shop, its walls
lined with mirrors; below, the
terrace room. Space is defined by rows
of banners, stiffened by battens,
which fit into coves that are planned
as part of the structure. Interior
design in a Portman building is part
of the concept from the beginning,
permitting this integration
of structure and decoration.

Above, a presentation in
progress in the large
meeting room at the top
of the hotel's base building.
Below, the ballroom.

Portman has retained control of the ownership of the building, so that he can always sell all or part of his equity if costs increase or he wishes to realize his investment immediately. Equity investors have different business purposes from those of a joint-venture partner like Trammell Crow. They seek tax shelter and an assured long-term return. Their aims are in accord with Portman's own business philosophy, which is more institutional in nature.

The completed hotel retains the simplicity of Portman's original design concept; it is essentially a round peg in a square hole. The round peg is the seventy-story cylindrical tower, clad in reflecting glass. The top three floors are given over to a revolving restaurant and cocktail lounge; then there are the fifty-six floors of bedrooms. The views are spectacular. The hotel is the tallest building in Atlanta, and it stands on the highest point in the central area of the city. Actually, the hotel turns out to be the tallest hotel structure in the world at the present time, and Western International is using this fact in its promotion. Portman did not seek the height for its own sake; it is a by-product of his original conceptual decision. Once he had decided to put all the rooms into a single compact tower, the height followed automatically from the market analysis and the economics of hotel operation, which dictated the number of rooms. The square hole, actually a rectangle, is a terraced opening in the seven-story base building, an understated concrete block designed to blend inconspicuously with the other commercial buildings fronting on Peachtree Street. This low building contains the ballrooms, meeting rooms, specialty restaurants, and major public spaces of the hotel.

While the concept can be described in simple terms, its elaboration into architecture has produced spaces of great complexity and interest. The architectural drama that people have come to expect from Portman is created by the process through which the round peg enters the rectangular hole. The mirrored sides of the tower appear to rest on a two-story concrete collar (containing meeting rooms), whose bottom edge is about 30 feet above the roof level of the base building. Below the collar all the rooms of the tower are stripped away, leaving only the supporting column structure, some narrow balcony walkways, and the elevator core. The opening in the base building that receives the tower is terraced, so that it is wider at the top. The space surrounding the tower within the base building is roofed with plexiglass domed skylights set in a steel frame structure. Because of the transition from circle to rectangle, these skylights form a warped plane, although this fact is not readily apparent from inside the building or from the street. If you go up to the swimming pool level on the roof, however, and look out over the roof of the main space, you see that it has a curious, reptilian appearance.

The floor of the main space is covered by a reflecting pool, which the hotel's advertising refers to as a half-acre lake. The tower is connected to the rest of the building by bridges at each level, and, at the base of the tower, boat-shaped islands are pushed out between the columns, forming places to have a drink and observe the space and the people.

Access to the rooftop restaurant is by two elevators that run in a glassed-in tube up the exterior of the tower. These elevators are entered at the fifth level, and the elevator structure is supported by a single cylindrical column that comes down into one quadrant of the main space. Another similar elevator structure on the opposite side of the building gives access to the meeting rooms located in the "collar."

The Peachtree Street entrance to the hotel leads you down a very long and narrow corridor, with shops opening off it on either side. The corridor is actually a bridge, and you can look down from it and catch glimpses of the space below, but it is deliberately extremely constricted. At the end of this entrance corridor is a wall, hung with a tapestry, that acts as a baffle. Only when you walk around this wall do you find yourself on a terrace, one level above the lake, looking out into the main space.

The motor entrance on the opposite side of the hotel is two floors lower, as the grade drops sharply away from Peachtree Street. From the motor entrance, an escalator brings you up facing the reception desk. You don't catch a glimpse of the water, and the large space opening up above it, until you turn away from the desk.

The exterior of the hotel is most impressive from a distance; the cylindrical mirrored tower dominates the Atlanta skyline. The three restaurant floors near the top have bronze-tinted windows rather than the reflecting glass that covers the mechanical floor above and the bedroom floors below. The strip of nonreflecting glass makes a subtle termination for the tower, giving something of the feeling of a band of ornament at the top of a column.

The hotel has been a great success from the day it opened, with its rooms operating at high occupancy rates and its restaurants and public areas filled with people. Portman has demonstrated again that spaces of real architectural distinction can be an important factor in a good commercial investment.

Portman's performance as a businessman has to be evaluated in terms of his whole organization. He does not always get the highest possible profit in early returns; he is investing for long-term gain because he feels that he is building for posterity as well as meeting the needs of the moment. However, he is also making profits from his architectural firm, his contract furnishings business, the marts, his management company, and so on. He is willing to take risks, but he seeks stability, safety, and long-term benefit.

As stated in Part 1, the clearest way to visualize the Portman organization is a circle with Portman in the center and the various components arranged chronologically in the order in which they are needed during the building birth cycle. It is a highly personal arrangement, much more an architectural office running a business than the other way around.

There are six people besides Portman whose responsibilities could be described as general. They provide administrative coordination of the architectural and engineering work and supervision of special areas like real estate finance, legal agreements, and the financial management of all Portman companies. There are several dozen other people in various parts of the organization who have important specific responsibilities: the presidents of Portman companies like Peachtree Center and Peachtree Purchasing and the heads of regional offices and of specialized services like interior design.

Portman's organization is not hierarchical; he will deal directly with any of these dozens of people on matters that concern them. However, if one of them runs into a problem, he will call on one of his six closest associates to help straighten it out. If the problem is at all serious, Portman will be involved as well.

Portman likes to work with a single designer on each project, and that designer continues to be involved all the way through the development process. Lately he has taken to working in this way with his son Jack, who entered the firm after receiving his master of architecture degree from Harvard in 1974.

Portman expects to be able to talk to any member of his organization and have the conversation repeated to any other staff member who needs to know about it. He refuses to deal in formalized lines of responsibility.

Members of his staff work together remarkably harmoniously, considering that their responsibilities overlap and that they must compete with each other for Portman's time and attention. Portman requires ultimate control, but he is also dependent on the colleagues who work with him. His is an organization based on strong personal relationships. Portman is the conceptualist and designer; his staff provides the necessary backup and technical support.

(See chart overleaf.)

What is the significance of Portman's work and business organization for other architects and real estate developers? Portman's initial success was very much tied to Atlanta in the booming 1950s and 1960s. It is unlikely that anyone else could repeat the same career today. He himself now designs and invests in a different way from the patterns he followed when he was getting started. Portman asserts that any architect can do what he did, but he is an unusual person who combines design ability with the temperament necessary to take the risks of real estate development. Perhaps only a small number of architects will prove willing and able to follow his example directly.

However, by demonstrating the mutual reinforcement between architecture and real estate, Portman has shown that architects ought to know a great deal more about finance and that developers, lenders, and investors have a lot to learn about architecture. If these professions would meet each other halfway instead of operating at cross-purposes, the results would be a great improvement over the way in which the environment is shaped today.

Architects who consider real estate finance to be crass and vulgar and beneath the notice of an artist should ask themselves if they are not cut off from some of the important roots of their art. Art generally requires artists to be masters of the medium in which they work. Can architects really master their art if they fail to understand the mechanism that makes so many buildings possible?

As Lewis Mumford once wrote, "The task of the original artist today, and in essence it is the same in literature, in philosophy and in architecture, is to bring 'science' and 'poetry' together again, for the knowledge that brings only power is brutal, and the culture which isolates itself from the sources of power is futile." [1]

[1] Lewis Mumford, "The Social Background of Frank Lloyd Wright," in *The Work of Frank Lloyd Wright,* Wendingen edition, republished by Bramhall House, New York, 1965, p. 79.

ARCHITECTURE

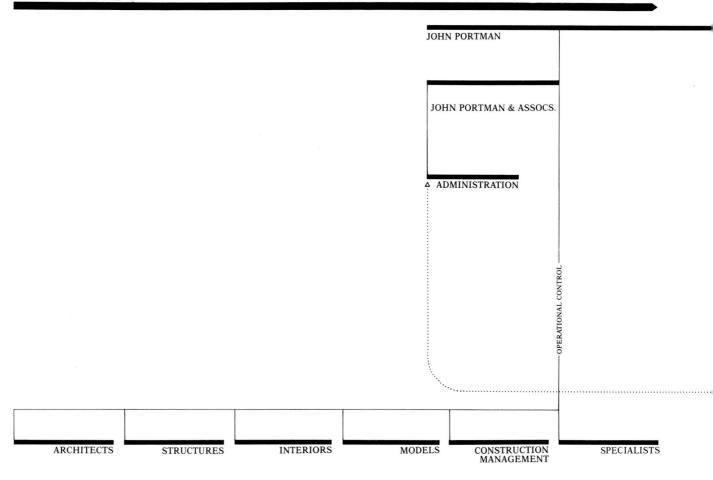

JOHN PORTMAN

JOHN PORTMAN & ASSOCS.

△ ADMINISTRATION

OPERATIONAL CONTROL

ARCHITECTS STRUCTURES INTERIORS MODELS CONSTRUCTION MANAGEMENT SPECIALISTS

ARCHITECTURAL PROCESS

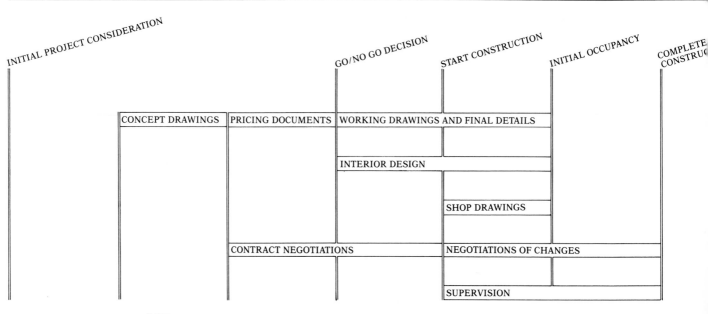

INITIAL PROJECT CONSIDERATION

GO/NO GO DECISION

START CONSTRUCTION

INITIAL OCCUPANCY

COMPLETE CONSTRUC

CONCEPT DRAWINGS | PRICING DOCUMENTS | WORKING DRAWINGS AND FINAL DETAILS

INTERIOR DESIGN

SHOP DRAWINGS

CONTRACT NEGOTIATIONS

NEGOTIATIONS OF CHANGES

SUPERVISION

188

DEVELOPMENT

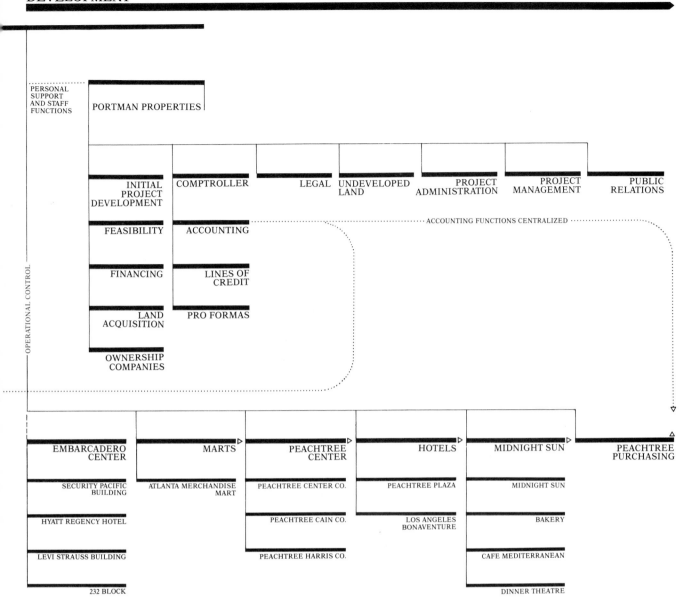

PERSONAL
SUPPORT
AND STAFF
FUNCTIONS

PORTMAN PROPERTIES

OPERATIONAL CONTROL

| INITIAL PROJECT DEVELOPMENT | COMPTROLLER | LEGAL | UNDEVELOPED LAND | PROJECT ADMINISTRATION | PROJECT MANAGEMENT | PUBLIC RELATIONS |

FEASIBILITY — ACCOUNTING

ACCOUNTING FUNCTIONS CENTRALIZED

FINANCING — LINES OF CREDIT

LAND ACQUISITION — PRO FORMAS

OWNERSHIP COMPANIES

| EMBARCADERO CENTER | MARTS | PEACHTREE CENTER | HOTELS | MIDNIGHT SUN | PEACHTREE PURCHASING |

SECURITY PACIFIC BUILDING — ATLANTA MERCHANDISE MART — PEACHTREE CENTER CO. — PEACHTREE PLAZA — MIDNIGHT SUN

HYATT REGENCY HOTEL — PEACHTREE CAIN CO. — LOS ANGELES BONAVENTURE — BAKERY

LEVI STRAUSS BUILDING — PEACHTREE HARRIS CO. — CAFE MEDITERRANEAN

232 BLOCK — DINNER THEATRE

DEVELOPMENT PROCESS

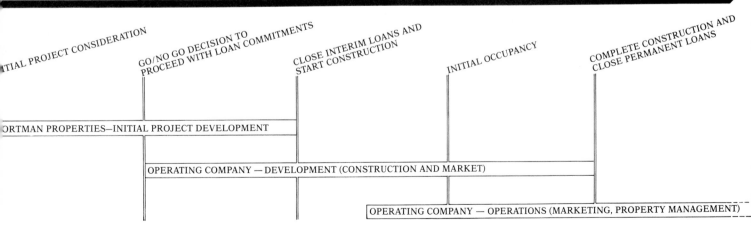

INITIAL PROJECT CONSIDERATION

GO/NO GO DECISION TO PROCEED WITH LOAN COMMITMENTS

CLOSE INTERIM LOANS AND START CONSTRUCTION

INITIAL OCCUPANCY

COMPLETE CONSTRUCTION AND CLOSE PERMANENT LOANS

PORTMAN PROPERTIES—INITIAL PROJECT DEVELOPMENT

OPERATING COMPANY — DEVELOPMENT (CONSTRUCTION AND MARKET)

OPERATING COMPANY — OPERATIONS (MARKETING, PROPERTY MANAGEMENT)

John Portman takes the art of architecture seriously. His buildings are clearly concerned with the great architectural issues that are the subject of theological debates among critics and historians, such as the manipulation of spatial sequences or the articulation and expression of structure. However, Portman's slogan, "An architecture for people and not for things," is actually a controversial statement about architectural theory. He is saying that architects have been spending too much time worrying about what are, after all, matters of technique while stopping short of the really important decisions about the way people will experience and react to a building.

Portman's design philosophy takes for granted many of the issues that other architects are now discovering under the names of user orientation, urban sociology, and environmental psychology. Portman has been considering such questions for years, at least partly because the entrepreneurial nature of his buildings demands it. The requirement that each of his designs justify itself in the marketplace has clearly helped to give him a deeper insight into what people want and need.

To carry out his design concepts Portman has also learned how to control costs. He has learned where to spend his money and how to use no more than necessary.

Architects who visit Portman's buildings and kick and poke them after the friendly fashion of architects looking over one another's work will find exposed or painted concrete and hung ceilings. The money is not spent in making the whole building like a fine piece of furniture but on structure, large enclosed volumes, and well-designed fittings. Real estate developers should take note of the many different ways in which Portman creates increased value through design without necessarily raising costs at all. Consider the complex of office buildings at Peachtree Center. The most important design factors are the consistent arrangement of the buildings with their identical materials, the two sunken plazas, and the glass Shopping Gallery.

The office buildings are not expensive structures, and the uniformity that adds so much to the design concept actually saves money. The two plazas occupy what would otherwise be unrentable space and are no larger than they need to be to turn the surrounding basement area into prime commercial frontage. The Shopping Gallery is an interesting and pleasant space but not a large and extravagant one, and it takes a dead-end location and turns it into four floors of stores, a most profitable rental area for developers. The cost of the gallery is easily absorbed by the additional retail space created.

These stores are rentable because of Portman's coordinate design concept: their proximity to hotels, offices, the mart, and the dinner theater.

Similar observations could be made at Embarcadero Center, where increased revenue from shops more than covers the additional cost of burying the parking, while the three levels of shops provide a much livelier environment than the podium of garage space in other parts of the redevelopment area. The same principle is at work in other Portman projects. Portman's phrase to describe it is "I never do anything for only one reason." He added a dinner theater to Peachtree Center to create a better architectural relationship between the buildings, but the theater also brings people into the center at night

190

and reinforces the hotels and the marts by providing a place to hold meetings in the daytime. Like most Portman enterprises, the dinner theater also is a successful business in its own right.

Why does not this coordination and reinforcement between architectural design and real estate development take place more often?

Why can't architect-developers or architect-developer teams become the coordinators of the built environment?

As John Portman says, it is not all that difficult.

A chronology of completed buildings designed by John C. Portman, Jr.

1953–1956   John C. Portman, Jr.
1956–1968   Edwards and Portman
1969–present John Portman and Associates

DATE	NAME	LOCATION	OWNER
1953	Fraternal Order of Eagles	Atlanta	Fraternal Order of Eagles
1954	Office building	Atlanta	Dr. Charles T. Henderson
1955	Residence	Atlanta	Mr. Sam Lemer
1955	Residence	Atlanta	Mr. R. Toubman
1956	Midway Elementary School	De Kalb County, Georgia	De Kalb County Board of Education
1957	Executive suite	Atlanta (Hurt Building)	Southern Bell
1957	Doctor's clinic and drugstore	Marietta, Georgia	Dr. Robert Coggins
1957	Oglethorpe Demonstration School	Atlanta	City of Atlanta
1958	Jeff Davis Elementary School addition	Hazelhurst, Georgia	Jeff Davis County
1959	YMCA Building	Southwest Atlanta	Young Men's Christian Association, Metropolitan Atlanta
1959	YMCA Building	West Side Atlanta	Young Men's Christian Association, Metropolitan Atlanta
1960	YMCA Building	Decatur, Georgia	Young Men's Christian Association, Metropolitan Atlanta
1960	Atlanta Merchandise Mart	Atlanta	Atlanta Merchandise Mart, Inc.
1960	Carey Reynolds Elementary School	Doraville, Georgia	De Kalb County Board of Education
1961	Infirmary Building	Georgia Institute of Technology, Atlanta	Georgia State Board of Regents
1961	YMCA Building	Rome, Georgia	Young Men's Christian Association, Metropolitan Atlanta
1961	Atlanta Decorative Arts Center	Atlanta	ADAC
1962	Jamestown Shopping Center	College Park, Georgia	Jamestown Shopping Center, Inc.
1962	Hawthorne Elementary School	Atlanta	De Kalb County Board of Education
1962	Fairburn High School addition	Fulton County, Georgia	Fulton County Board of Education
1963	Atlanta Plant addition	Atlanta	Pollack Paper Co.
1963	Perry Homes addition	Atlanta	Atlanta Housing Authority
1963	Sequoyah High School	Doraville, Georgia	De Kalb County Board of Education
1963	Hawthorne School addition	Atlanta	De Kalb County Board of Education
1964	Portman residence	Atlanta	J. C. Portman, Jr.
1964	Sequoyah High School addition	Doraville, Georgia	De Kalb County Board of Education

1964	Trailways Garage and Parking Deck	Atlanta	Smoky Mountain Stages, Inc.
1964	Pollack Plant addition	Birmingham, Alabama	Pollack Paper Co.
1965	Greenbriar Shopping Center	Atlanta	W. R. Hawn
1965	Service Center School	Atlanta	City of Atlanta
1965	Peachtree Center Building (230)	Atlanta	Peachtree Center Company
1965	Antoine Graves Houses	Atlanta	Atlanta Housing Authority
1965	Dana Fine Arts Center	Decatur, Georgia	Agnes Scott College
1965	Herndon Elementary School	Atlanta	Atlanta Board of Education
1965	Herndon Elementary School addition	Atlanta	Atlanta Board of Education
1965	Sequoyah High School addition	De Kalb County, Georgia	De Kalb County Board of Education
1965	Hawthorne School addition	Atlanta	De Kalb County Board of Education
1965	Greenbriar Tire Center	Atlanta	Rich's Tire Center
1965	Greenbriar First National Bank	Atlanta	First National, Atlanta
1965	Greenbriar Rich's	Atlanta	Rich's, Inc.
1965	Greenbriar Theater	Atlanta	Greenbriar Shopping Center Company
1965	Trailways Temporary Terminal	Atlanta	Trailways Bus, Inc.
1966	Spalding Drive Elementary School	Atlanta	Fulton County Board of Education
1966	One Peachtree Street Building (alteration and addition)	Atlanta	Smith, Pope, Carter Co.
1966	Sequoyah High School addition	Doraville, Georgia	De Kalb County Board of Education
1966	Midway Elementary School	Decatur, Georgia	De Kalb County Board of Education
1966	Carey Reynolds School addition	Doraville, Georgia	De Kalb County Board of Education
1966	Pollack Paper addition	Atlanta	Pollack Realty
1967	Regency Hyatt Hotel	Atlanta	Hyatt Corp.
1967	C. W. Hill School	Atlanta	Atlanta Public Schools
1967	Henderson High School	Chamblee, Georgia	De Kalb County Board of Education
1967	Spalding Drive School addition	Fulton County, Georgia	Fulton County Board of Education
1968	Atlanta Merchandise Mart addition	Atlanta	Atlanta Merchandise Mart Corporation
1968	Gas Light Tower	Atlanta	Peachtree Center Company
1968	Trailways Bus Terminal	Atlanta	Conbus Corp.
1968	Midnight Sun restaurant	Atlanta	Midnight Sun, Inc.

1968	Henderson High School addition	Atlanta	De Kalb County Board of Education
1969	Midway Elementary School addition	Decatur, Georgia	De Kalb County Board of Education
1969	ADAC addition	Atlanta	Atlanta Decorative Arts Center
1969	Henderson High School addition	Atlanta	De Kalb County Board of Education
1970	ADAC addition	Atlanta	Atlanta Decorative Arts Center
1970	Peachtree Center South Building	Atlanta	C. P. Company
1971	J. F. Kennedy School and Community Center	Atlanta	City of Atlanta Board of Education
1971	Chicago Hyatt Hotel	Chicago O'Hare	Hyatt Corp.
1971	Hyatt Regency Atlanta addition	Atlanta	Hyatt Corp.
1971	Blue Cross Office Building	Chattanooga, Tennessee	Blue Cross–Blue Shield of Tennessee
1971	Alfred Blalock Elementary School	Atlanta	City of Atlanta Board of Education
1971	John Portman Associates office interior design	Atlanta	John Portman and Associates
1971	Dallas Office Building (eight-story)	Dallas	Park Central Company
1971	Dallas Office Building (nine-story)	Dallas	Park Central Company
1971	Security Pacific National Bank	San Francisco	Embarcadero Center Associates
1974	Peachtree Cain Building	Atlanta	Peachtree Cain Co.
1974	Hyatt Regency Hotel	San Francisco	Embarcadero Center Associates
1974	Levi Strauss Building (231)	San Francisco	Embarcadero Center Associates
1974	Fort Worth National Bank	Fort Worth, Texas	Fort Worth National Bank
1975	Shopping Gallery	Atlanta	Peachtree Cain Co.
1975	Brussels World Trade Mart	Brussels	Brussels International Trade Mart, Ltd.
1976	Embarcadero Center (232)	San Francisco	Embarcadero Center Associates
1976	Peachtree Center Plaza Hotel	Atlanta	Peachtree Hotel Co.
1976	Peachtree Harris Tower	Atlanta	Peachtree Harris Co.

UNDER CONSTRUCTION:

	Bonaventure Hotel	Los Angeles	Los Angeles Portman Company
	Renaissance Center	Detroit	Renaissance Center partnership

Illustration credits

All photographs were taken specially for this book by Jerry Spearman, with the following exceptions:

The model photographs are by Clyde May, except for the photograph on page 50, which is by Gerald Ratto. The photograph on page 11 is by James Amos, the photographs of furniture on page 17 are by Robin Johnstone and Bruce Dell, the photograph on page 23 is by Edgar Orr, page 27 (top) is by Arno Wrubel, pages 28 and 82 (bottom) are by William Barnes, and pages 38 (top), 69, 75, 87, 88, 97, 107, and 122 are by Alexandre Georges. The photograph on page 42 is used by courtesy of the Brussels International Mart, and the photomontages on pages 50 and 133 by courtesy of the Ford Motor Company.

All drawings and all other photomontages are by John Portman & Associates.

Acknowledgments

The authors wish to thank John Street, Mickey Steinberg, Herbert Lembcke, Charles Daoust, and Travis Brannon for reviewing various drafts of the manuscript and making many helpful suggestions. We are grateful to John Ottley and Donald Cutler for their advice, Judy Perry for keeping everything together, Maxine Wells and Frances Gretes for research, Peter Polites for his work on the drawings, and Darlene Bledsoe and Pat Garasic for typing and retyping the manuscript.

195

Index